THE BEST-EVER PAPER PLANE CHALLENGE

Discover how to make four awesome planes and get ready for *The Best-ever Paper Plane Challenge!* There are 10 cool illustrated designs for each type of plane, which are designed to fly accurately and straight for long distances: perfect for all sorts of competitive games and challenges. There are 8 fun games for you to try, tear-out score sheets to keep track of your successes, plus targets, a hangar and a runway!

Paper plane challenges have been around for a while; the first international paper plane competition was held in 1967. The competition brought together various styles and forms of paper plane making from all over the world. In December 2010, Takuo Toda set the Guinness World Record for longest paper plane time aloft with a time of 29.2 seconds!

Contents

Glossary 2–3
Folding steps 4–12
Games 13–16
Illustrated Plane Designs 17–96
Scoring Sheets 97–112

TO MAKE THE HANGAR

Fold the tops of the walls over and fasten the roof by using the tabs. Attach the triangular gable to the front of the hangar using the tabs; this will support the roof.

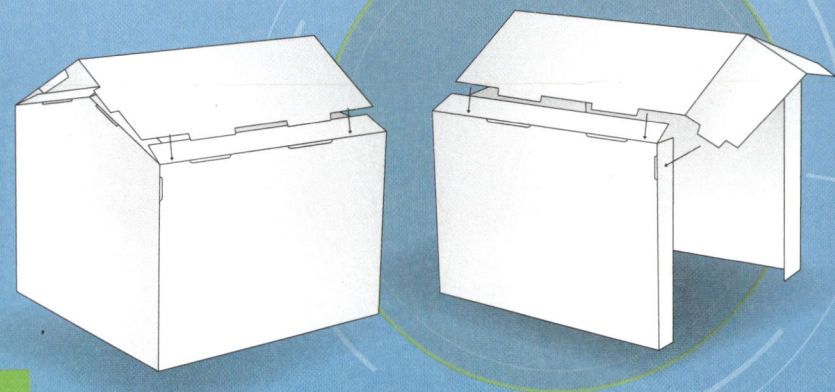

ABOUT THE AUTHOR

Dean Mackey has always enjoyed flying paper planes. Some of his earliest memories are of flying paper planes off the porch and over the cliff across the street. As well as experimenting with his own designs, Dean started collecting web links that talented people had put online for all to enjoy. A few years later, he launched The Online Paper Airplane Museum, featuring over 800 free paper plane designs, reviews of paper plane books, and other paper planes items. Visit The Online Paper Airplane Museum at **http://www.theonlinepaperairplanemuseum.com**. Questions or comments can be sent to Dean at **deanmackey@gmail.com**. Dean's comments on the various plane designs are mentioned throughout.

AVIATION GLOSSARY

AILERON
A movable panel at the rear edge of each aeroplane wing; the aileron can be raised or lowered and cause the plane to bank left or right.

AIRFOIL
The shape of the wing as seen from the side; it is the shape of the wing that causes a plane to lift.

CANARD
A small wing that sits forward of the main wings on the fuselage of a plane.

DIHEDRAL
The position of the wings on a plane relative to the fuselage. If the wings are raised relative to the fuselage, the dihedral is positive. If the wings are lowered, the dihedral is negative.

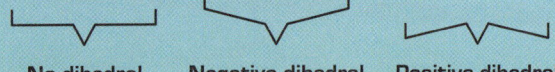

No dihedral   Negative dihedral   Positive dihedral

ELEVATOR
The control flaps at the rear of an aircraft; the elevator can be raised or lowered and cause the plane to ascend or descend.

FUSELAGE
The main body of a plane; the wings and tail attach to the fuselage of the plane.

RUDDER
A vertical airfoil at the tail of a plane used for steering; the rudder can be moved left or right and cause the plane to move right or left.

SPOILER
A small airfoil, usually found on the rear of a racing car. On the planes in this book, a spoiler is intended to increase lift.

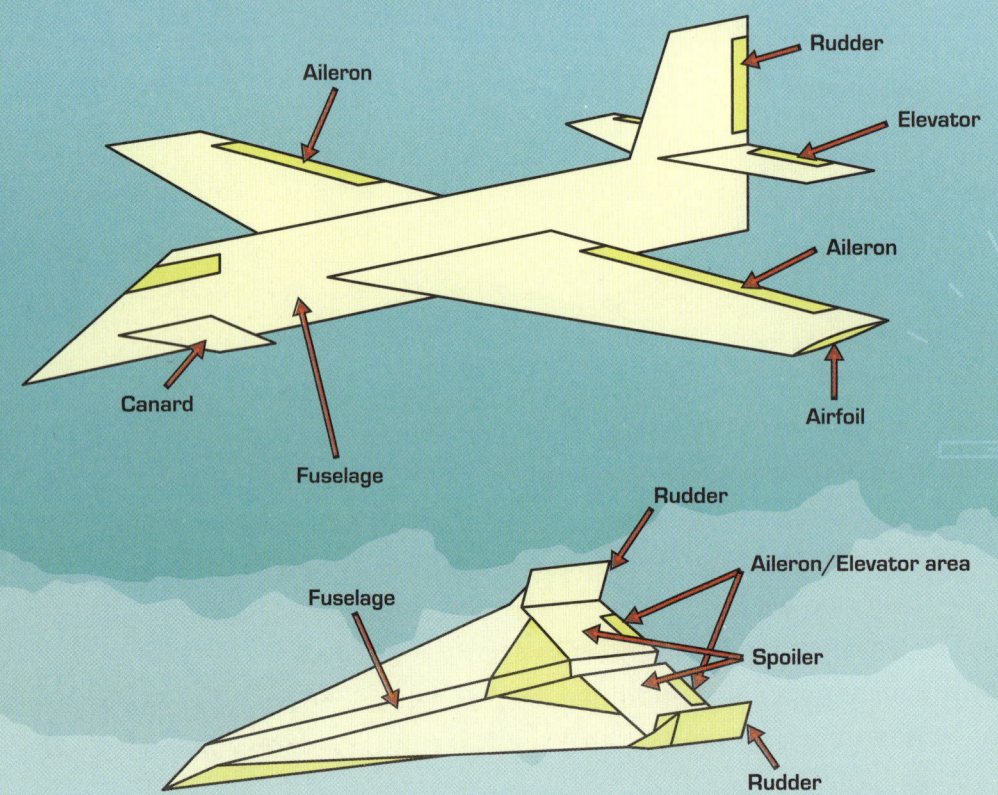

FOLDING GLOSSARY

Here are some folding terms that are commonly used when making paper planes.

FLIP FOLD
Fold up along the result of a previous fold.

INSIDE REVERSE FOLD
The corner of an existing fold is creased, pushed in and folded on the inside.

MOUNTAIN FOLD
Fold the sides together so the paper forms a ∧ shape.

PRESS
Use your fingers to push the paper in the correct direction.

PRESS FOLD
Bring two creases together and press down the excess paper that is curved between them to create a new crease.

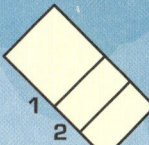  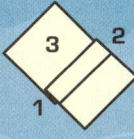

REVERSE FOLD
The corner of an existing fold is creased, reversed and folded over to the outside.

SQUASH FOLD
Start with at least two layers of paper. Make creases in the top layer. Lift the top layer, move it across and then press down on the creases.

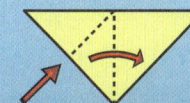 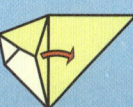 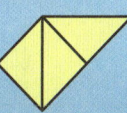

TAP
Use your finger and tap where indicated to set off a preset series of folds.

TRIM
The final adjustments to a paper plane so that it flies straight and true. This may involve adjustments to the ailerons, elevator and rudder.

VALLEY FOLD
Fold the sides together so the paper forms a V shape.

STANDARD

Here is a plane design that is truly international. I recently met a Russian woman who had made this in her childhood. It is exactly the same design I learned growing up in Iowa. Capable of fast speed and accuracy, the Standard will streak across the sky!

Begin with a sheet of A4 paper.

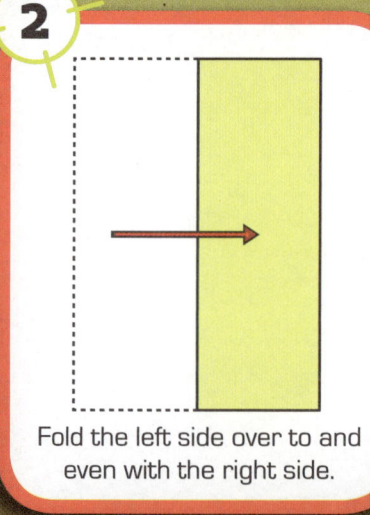

Fold the left side over to and even with the right side.

Fold the top right corner down to the left side.

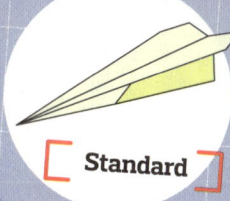
[Standard]

4
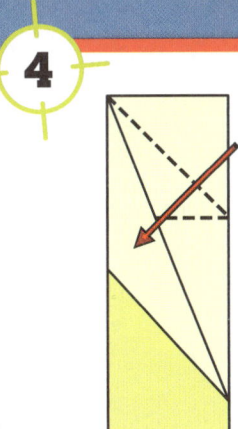
Fold the right side over to the left side as shown.

5
Fold again from the right side over to the left side as shown.

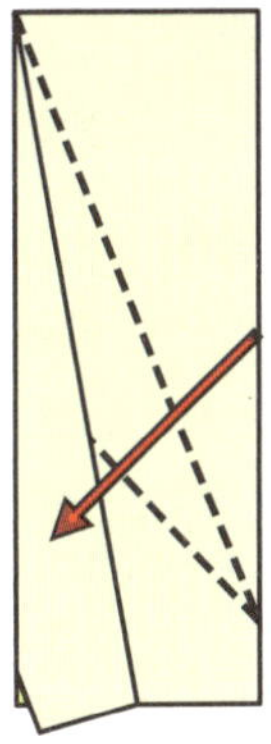

6
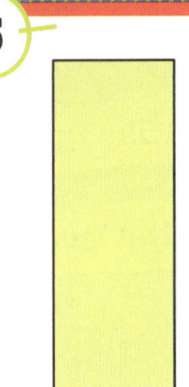
Flip over, from left to right.

7
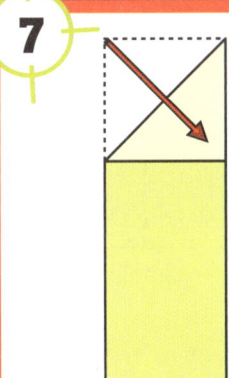
Fold the top left corner down to the right side.

8
Fold from the left side over to the right side as shown.

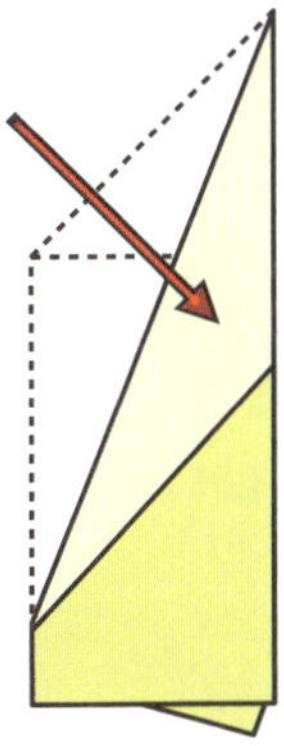

9

Fold the left side over to the right side again as shown.

UNFOLD AND POP UP THE WINGS TO GIVE A SLIGHT POSITIVE DIHEDRAL, AS SHOWN. THIS PLANE WILL FLY FAR AND FAST IF YOU GRASP IT ALONG THE FUSELAGE AND THROW IT AS HARD AS YOU CAN!

JAVELIN

Much like the track and field spear this plane is named after, the Javelin is truly meant for distance competitions.

1 Begin with a sheet of A4 paper.

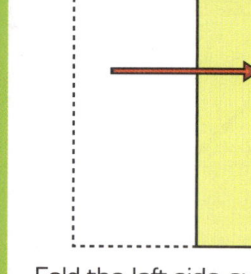
2 Fold the left side over to and even with the right side.

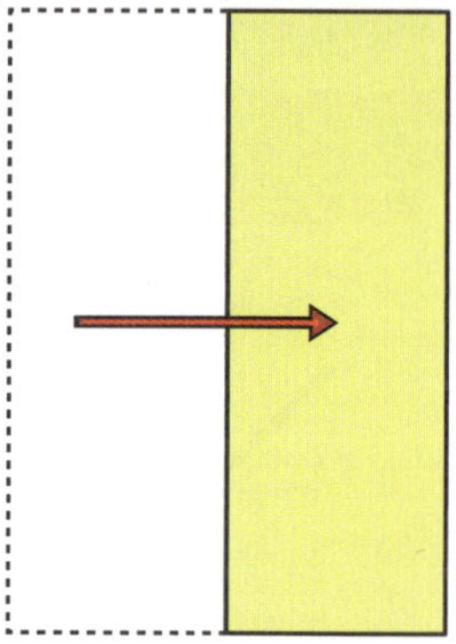

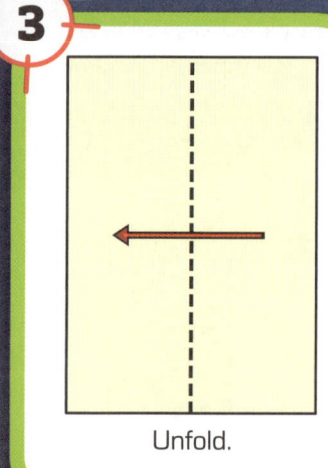
3 Unfold.

4 Fold the top left corner down.

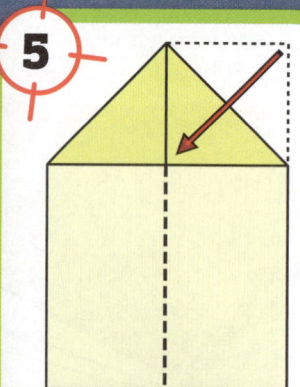
5 Repeat the same fold with the top right corner.

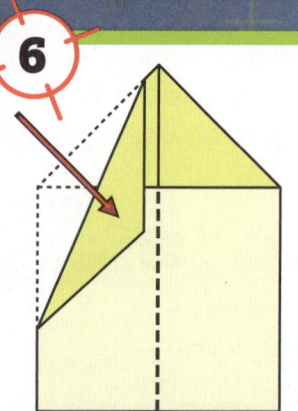
6 Fold the left side in, stopping 1.5 cm (0.6 inches) from the centre crease.

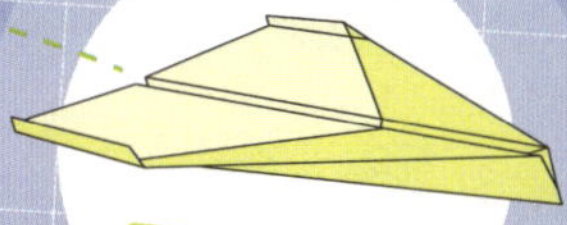

[Javelin]

7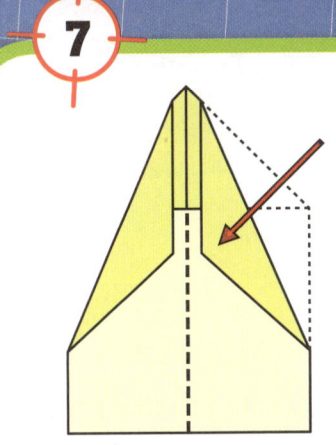
Repeat on the right side, stopping 1.5 cm (0.6 inches) from the centre crease.

8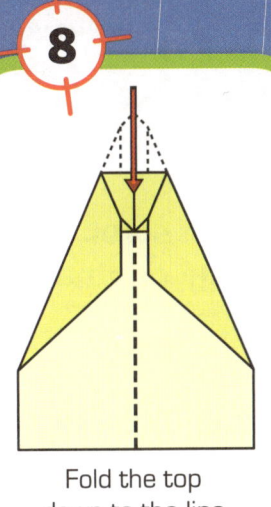
Fold the top down to the line as shown.

9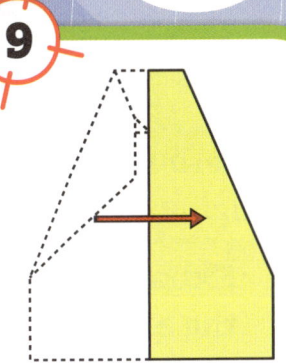
Fold the left side over to and even with the right side.

10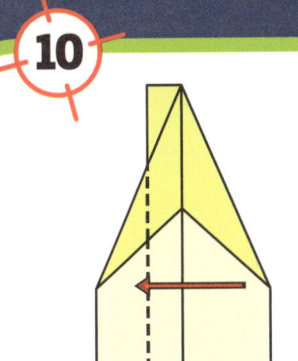
Fold the top wing to the left, starting at the top right corner and keeping the bottom edge even.

11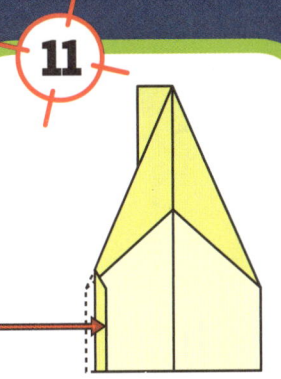
Fold the left side in 1 cm (0.4 inches).

12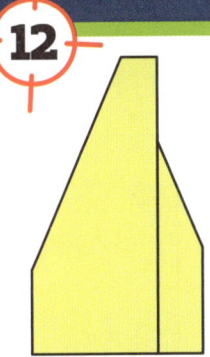
Flip over, from left to right.

13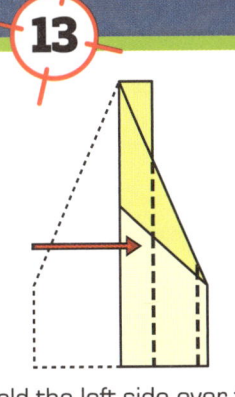
Fold the left side over to the right side, keeping the left edge even with the wing beneath it.

14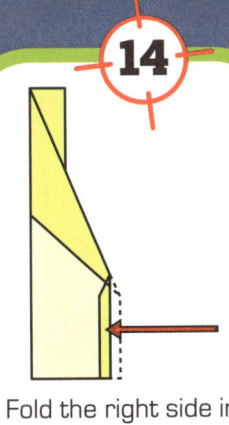
Fold the right side in 1 cm (0.4 inches).

THIS IS A GREAT AND GRACEFUL DISTANCE FLYER. IT MAY NEED A LITTLE UP ELEVATOR, BUT IN STILL AIR, THE JAVELIN WILL FLY STRAIGHT AND FAR!

AFTERBURNER

An afterburner is a component of some jet engines, placed after the main engine.

Extra fuel is injected into the afterburner and burned for increased thrust.

In this paper plane, a spoiler is placed near the end to increase lift. Adding the spoiler to the stabilisers also makes it more stable!

1

Begin with a sheet of A4 paper.

2
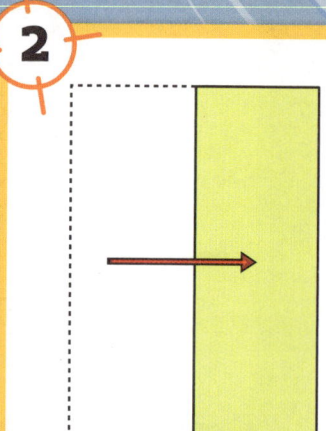
Fold the left side over to and even with the right side.

3
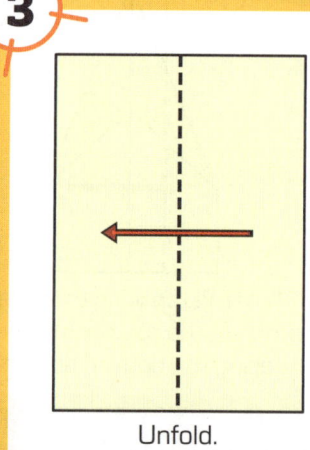
Unfold.

4
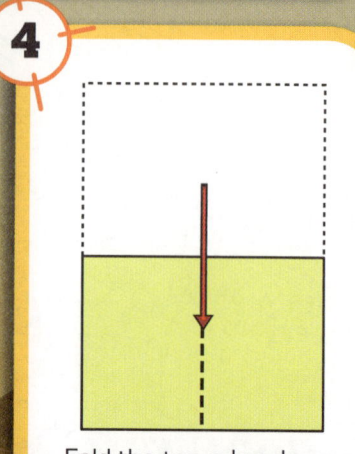
Fold the top edge down to the bottom edge.

5
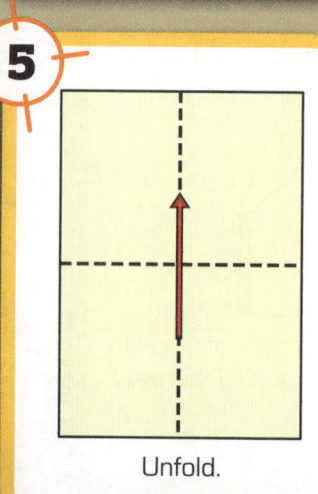
Unfold.

6
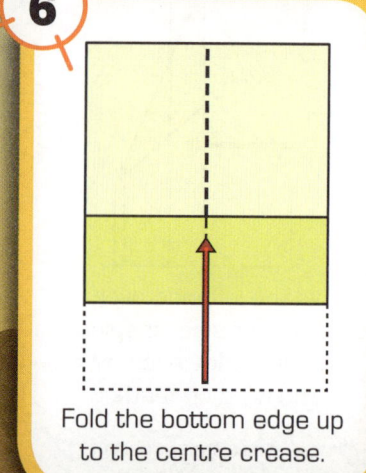
Fold the bottom edge up to the centre crease.

Afterburner

7
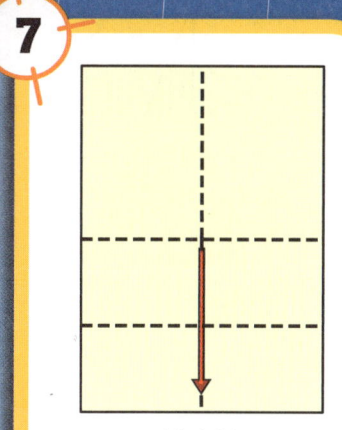
Unfold.

8
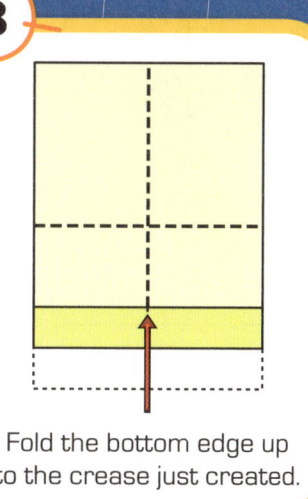
Fold the bottom edge up to the crease just created.

9
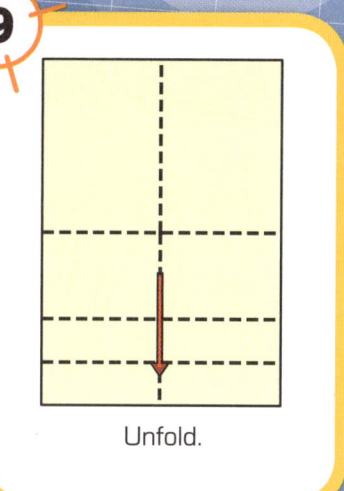
Unfold.

10
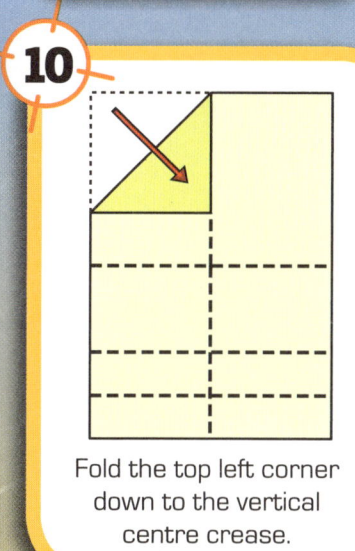
Fold the top left corner down to the vertical centre crease.

11
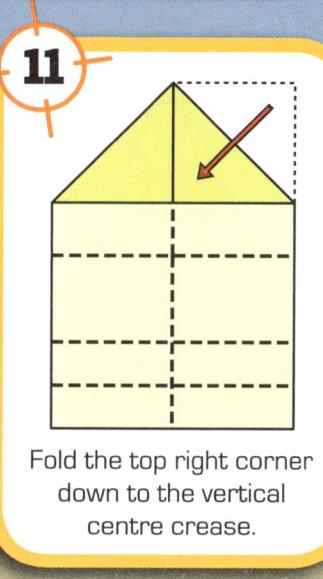
Fold the top right corner down to the vertical centre crease.

12
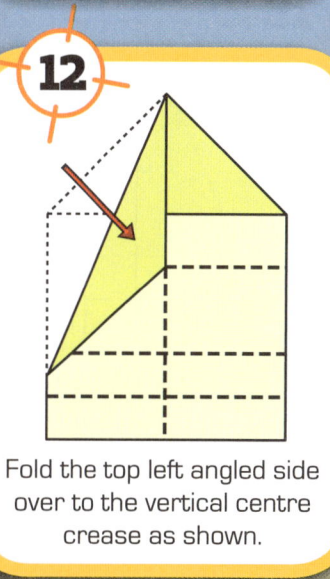
Fold the top left angled side over to the vertical centre crease as shown.

13
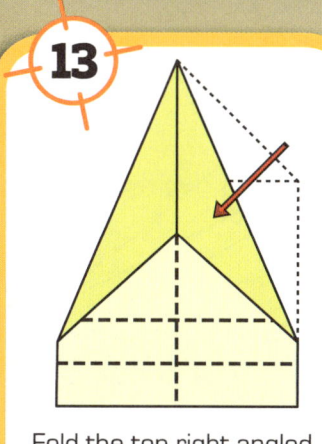
Fold the top right angled side over to the vertical centre crease as shown.

14
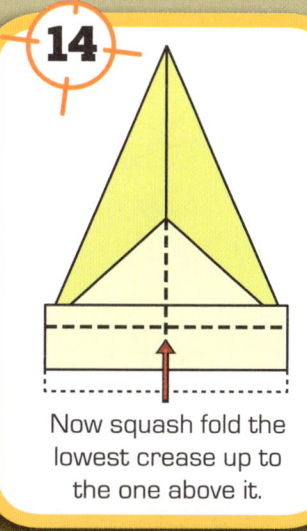
Now squash fold the lowest crease up to the one above it.

15
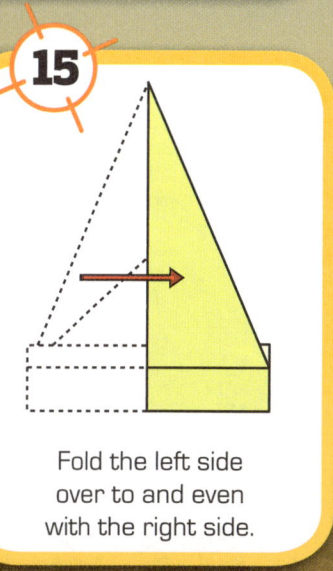
Fold the left side over to and even with the right side.

Afterburner

16

Fold the top wing over to the left, leaving 2 cm (0.8 inches) for the fuselage.

17

Fold the left side over 2.5 cm (1 inch).

18

Flip, from left to right.

19

Fold the left side over so that the left side on top matches the fold below.

20

Fold the right side over 2.5 cm (1 inch).

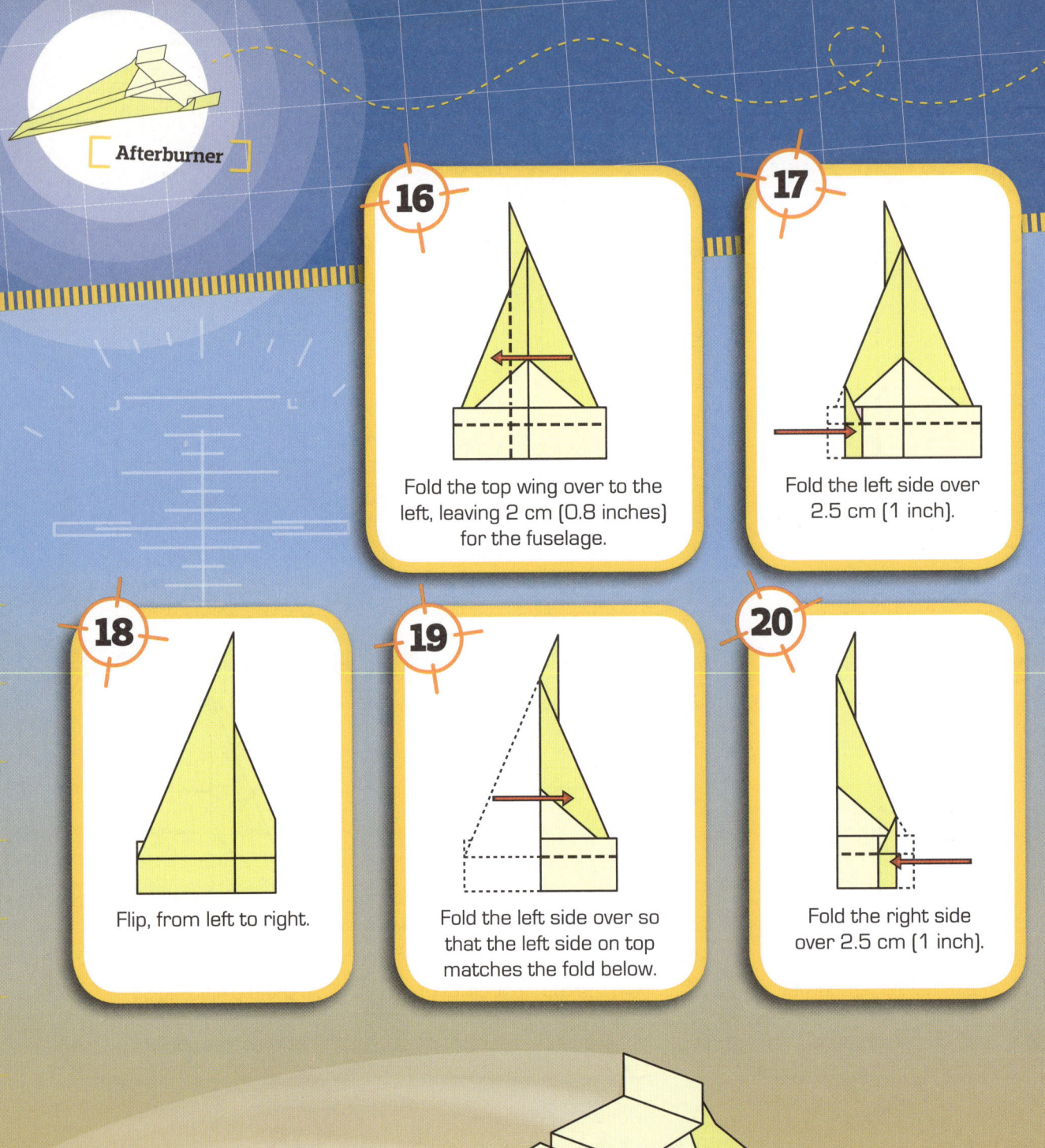

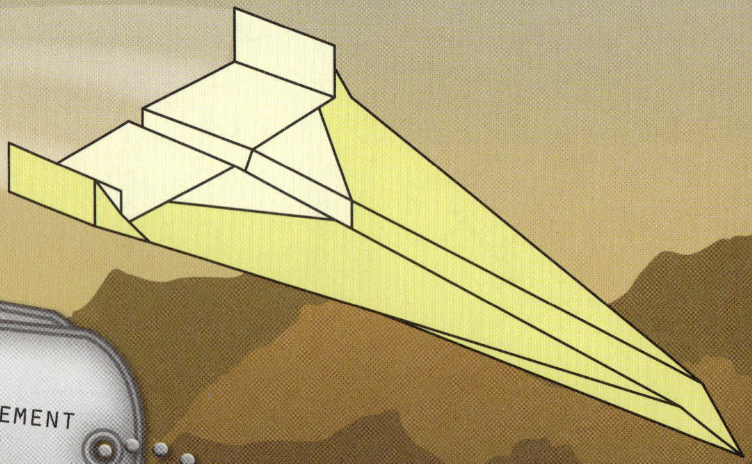

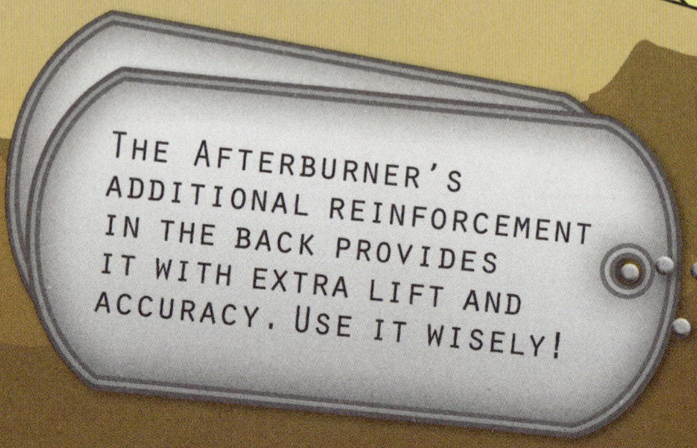

NAKAMURA LOCK

I only wish I had come up with this classic design myself.

I am still trying to find out who did so originally, as it appears in many books about paper planes.

The Nakamura Lock is a truly graceful flyer, and worth including in any paper-plane book!

1 Begin with a sheet of A4 paper.

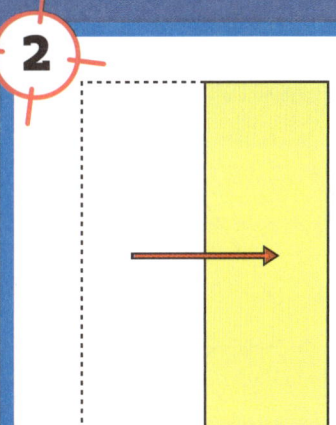
2 Fold the left side over to and even with the right side.

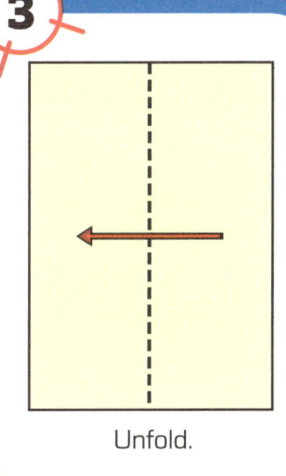
3 Unfold.

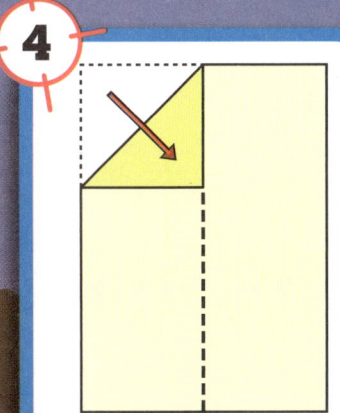
4 Fold the top left corner down to the centre crease as shown.

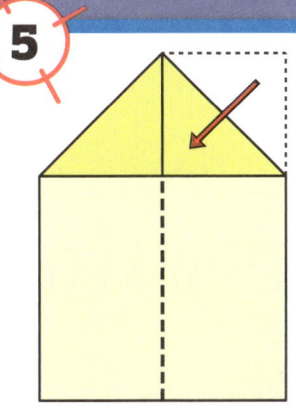
5 Fold the top right corner down to the centre crease as shown.

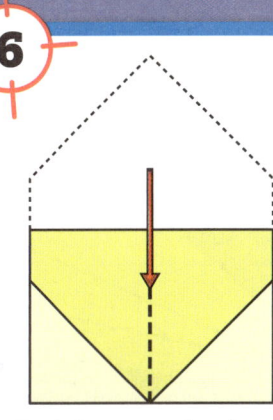
6 Fold the top point down to the bottom edge.

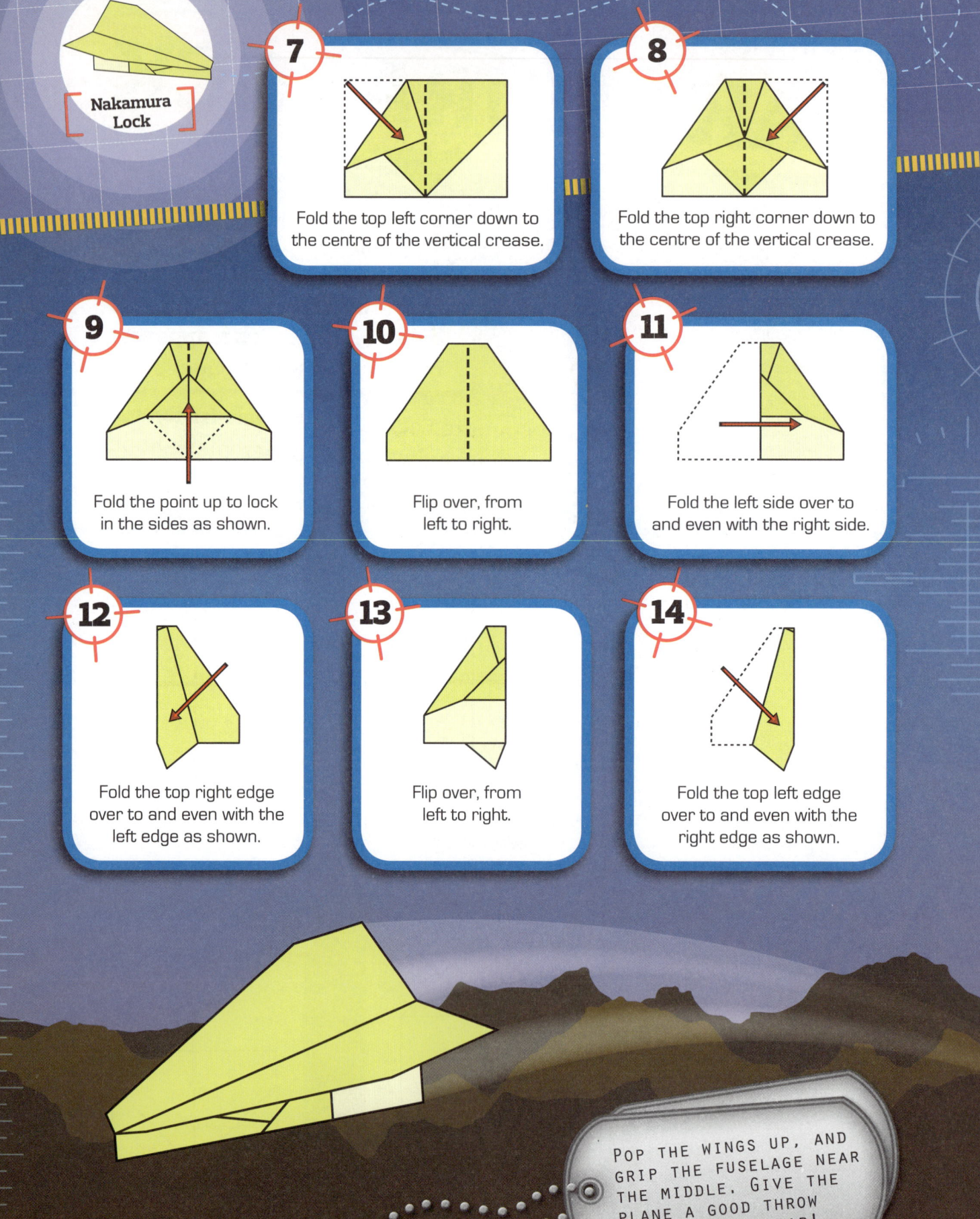

GAMES

[Games]

When you have perfected your paper planes, you can start using your creations to play some super-fun games!

For each of these games, we recommend starting five big steps (paces) away from the target, and then moving back a few paces as your skills improve. There is space within the score sheets to record how far back from the target you stood each game.

You can use whichever plane you like for these games, but you might like to start with the Standard plane, which is the easiest to use, and work through the others as you get better!

Most games are designed for two or more players, but most can also be played on your own, simply by trying to improve on your own scores, times and distances rather than against a friend. You can also change the length of most games, depending on how long you want to play, just by having ten turns each instead of five. There are score sheets provided for both options.

PLANE POOL

Players:
2 or more

What you need:
- Paper plane of choice (each)
- Large square of card or paper (A3 size or larger would be best)
- Coloured markers
- Blu Tack or masking tape
- Place marker, such as a coin or a strip of masking tape

Instructions:

On a large square of card, use markers to draw eight pool balls with the numbers 1-8 in different colours (ensuring the 8 ball is black, as per the picture shown). Try to make all of the balls the same size and shape.

Hang the card on a wall or door using the Blu Tack or masking tape (check with an adult that it won't mark the wall).

Place a marker on the ground five paces from the card. Each player should then take it in turns to try to hit each of the pool balls from 1 to 8 in ascending order. If a player hits the correct number, they get a second turn. If they miss the target completely their opponent gets two turns, and if a player hits the 8 ball before they have hit all the other seven balls in order, they lose – just like in real pool!

Tick off each ball hit (sunk) in the 'Plane Pool' score sheets provided.

HANG TIME

Players:
2 or more

What you need:
- Paper plane of choice (each)
- Stopwatch

Instructions:

Take it in turns to fly your planes, seeing how long you can keep them in the air. It will help if you have a high starting point to fly your plane from, such as a hill or a balcony.

Take five turns each, ensuring that you write your times in one of the score cards provided. The person with the longest time after 5 turns wins!

13

TRAFFIC-LIGHT BULLSEYE

Players:

2 or more

What you need:

- Paper plane of choice (each)
- Hanging target (supplied)
- Piece of string
- Place marker such as a coin or strip of masking tape

Instructions:

Pop the centre circles out of the target sheet. Put these aside for the game 'Target Practice'.

Tie one end of the string through the red hole at the top of the target and tie the other end around a hook, beam, tree branch or similar, so that the target dangles at around your head height or a little higher.

Place the place marker on the ground 5 paces from the target. Each player should then take it in turns to try to fly their plane through one of the holes. If a player gets a plane through the middle hole, they get 10 points. If the plane goes through the top or bottom hole, they get 5 points. If they hit the red, orange or green circles of the target they score 3 points, and if they hit the yellow back section they score 1 point.

Take 5 turns each, ensuring that you write your scores in one of the score sheets provided. The person with the most points after 5 turns wins!

EMERGENCY LANDING

Players:

2 or more

What you need:

- Paper plane of choice (each)
- Hangar (supplied)
- Runway (supplied)
- Place marker such as a coin or strip of masking tape

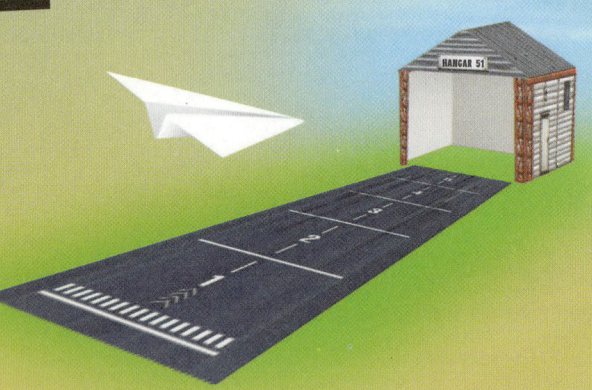

Instructions:

Set up the hangar as instructed at the start of this book. Place it on a flat surface such as a table, bench or footpath. Place the runway at the front of the hangar so that it meets at the doorway.

Place the place marker on the ground 5 paces from the target. Each player should then take it in turns to try to fly their plane along the runway and safely into the hangar. If a player gets their plane into the hangar, they score 10 points. If the plane lands on the runway, they score the number of points shown in the section that the plane's nose is touching. If the plane lands upside down, the player loses 3 points, and if they miss the runway altogether, they lose 1 point.

Take 5 turns each, ensuring that you write your scores in 1 of the score sheets provided. The person with the most points after 5 turns wins!

FURTHEST FLIGHT

Players:

2 or more

What you need:

- Paper plane of choice (each)
- Place marker, such as a coin or strip of masking tape

Instructions:

Put the place marker at the starting point so the players know where to stand for take-off. Line up beside each other and fly your planes as far as you can. It will help if you have a high starting point to fly your planes from, such as a hill or a balcony.

Each player should count out the distance in paces and write the distance in the score card. After five turns, the person with the highest total distance wins!

You might like to change the rules and make it so that the person with the longest individual flight is the winner!

DEMOLITION BOWLING

Players:

2

What you need:

- 3 paper planes of choice (each)
- 12 light items such as plastic figures, empty plastic bottles or dominoes
- Chalk or masking tape

Instructions:

Players should stand 10 paces apart in an open space, such as a playground, basketball court or field. Using chalk for a hard surface such as concrete, or masking tape for grass, each player should make a line on the ground about the width of an arm span.

Each player should stand behind their line, and line up the figures in front of the line. Each player starts with 3 planes each, and they must try to knock down the other player's figures. Each knocked-down figure is out of the game, but if a player catches their opponent's plane before it hits the ground, they may bring back 1 of their figures.

Players may run in between lines to collect planes that have landed, but may only throw their planes from behind their line. There is no taking turns – each player should throw as many planes as they can! The winner is the player who knocks down all of their opponent's figures first.

To play this game on your own, just line up 10 figurines like normal bowling pins, and try to knock them all down in one go!

Always be careful when throwing planes towards people. Never aim for the head or face.

TARGET PRACTICE

Players:
2 or more

What you need:
- 5 paper planes (each)
- 3 pop-out round targets

Instructions:
Place the target in the middle of a large space such as a playground or yard. Make sure there isn't too much wind around or your target will be a moving one!

Move 5 paces back from the target, and place a small stone or stick on the ground here to mark the starting position. Each player should then take it in turns to try to fly their planes closest to the target. The player who gets the closest to the target after everyone has had their turn, wins!

If you'd like to really test your skill, try placing the second target 2 or 3 paces further away than the first target, then repeat with the third target. That way, your challenge is to hit the centre of all 3 targets with only 5 planes!

A.I.R.P.O.R.T.

Players:
2 or more

What you need:
- Paper plane of choice (each)
- A hoop
- Rope or string
- Place-marker such as a coin or strip of masking tape

You can change the word 'AIRPORT' to anything you like. Why not try 'YOU ARE OUT' for a longer game?

Instructions:
Hang the hoop from a tree branch or beam using the rope or string so that it dangles at about your head height or just a little higher.

Place the place marker on the ground 5 paces from the target. The players should line up behind the marker in order of age, youngest first. Each player should then take it in turns to try to fly their plane through the hoop, then move to the back of the line. If a player gets their plane through the hoop, they are safe. If a player misses, they are given the letter 'A'. The next time they miss, they will be given the letter 'I', then 'R', 'P', 'O', 'R' and 'T'. When a player has been given all the letters of 'AIRPORT' they are out!

The winner is the last player still left in the game.

Standard

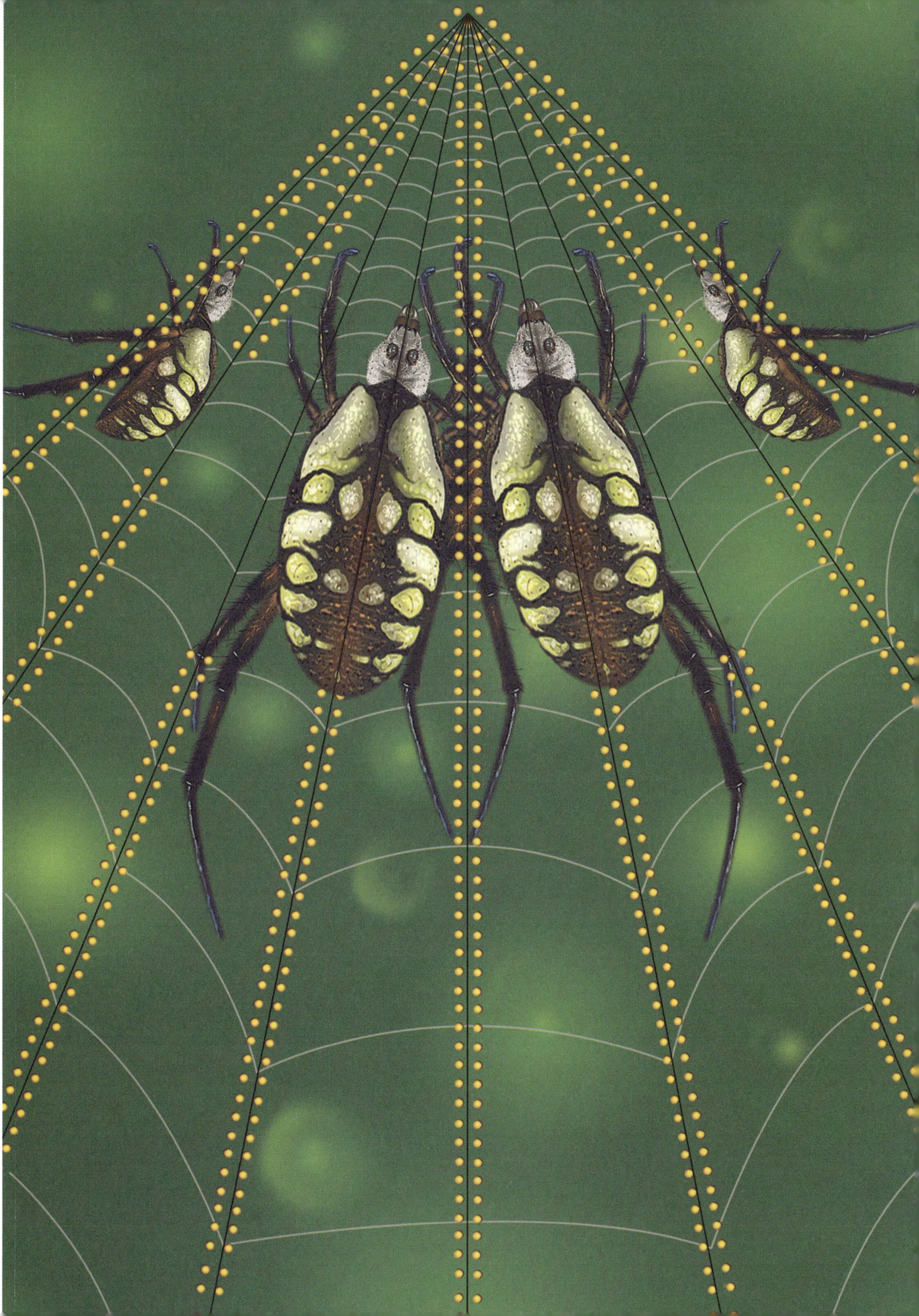

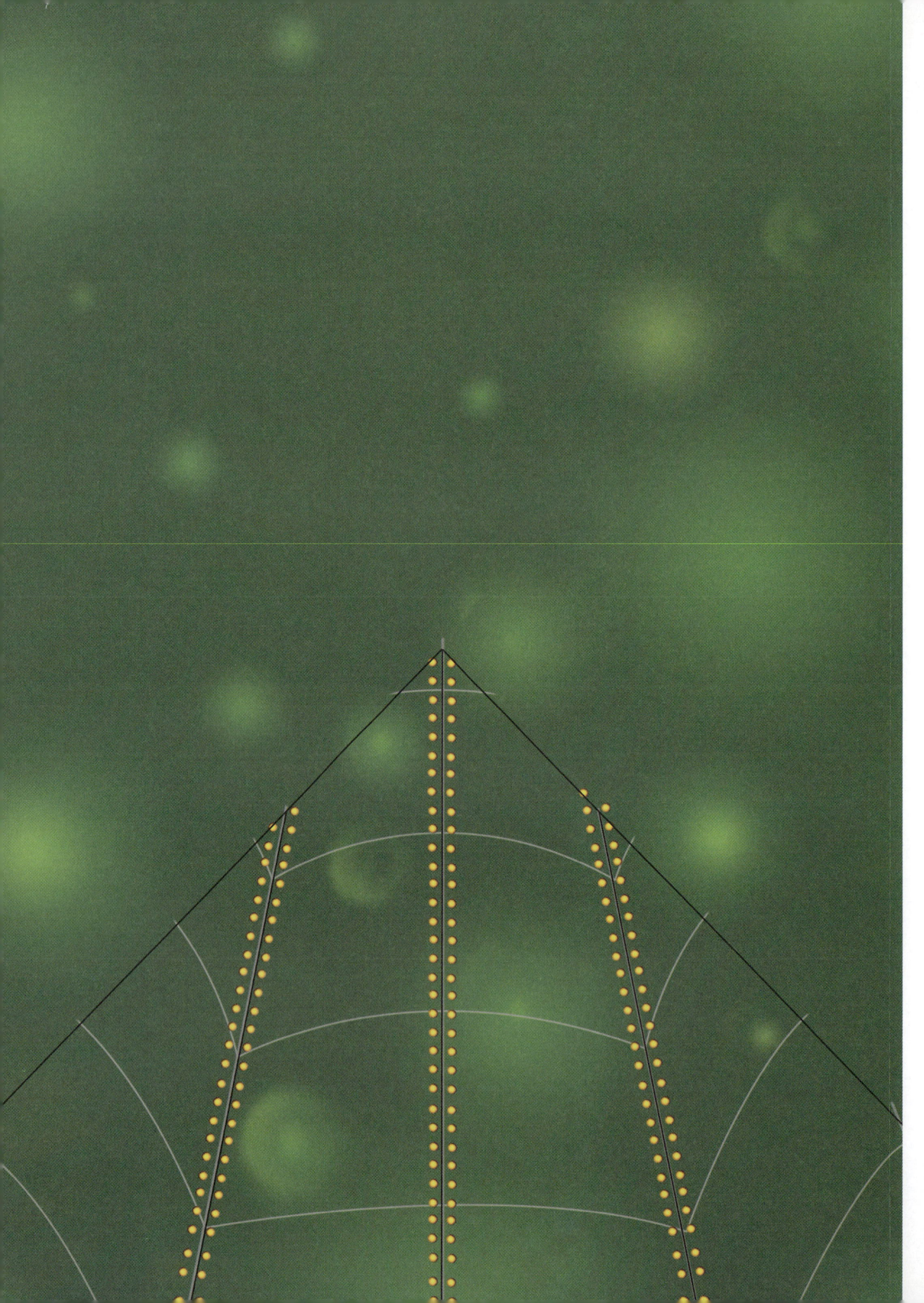

Standard

Javelin

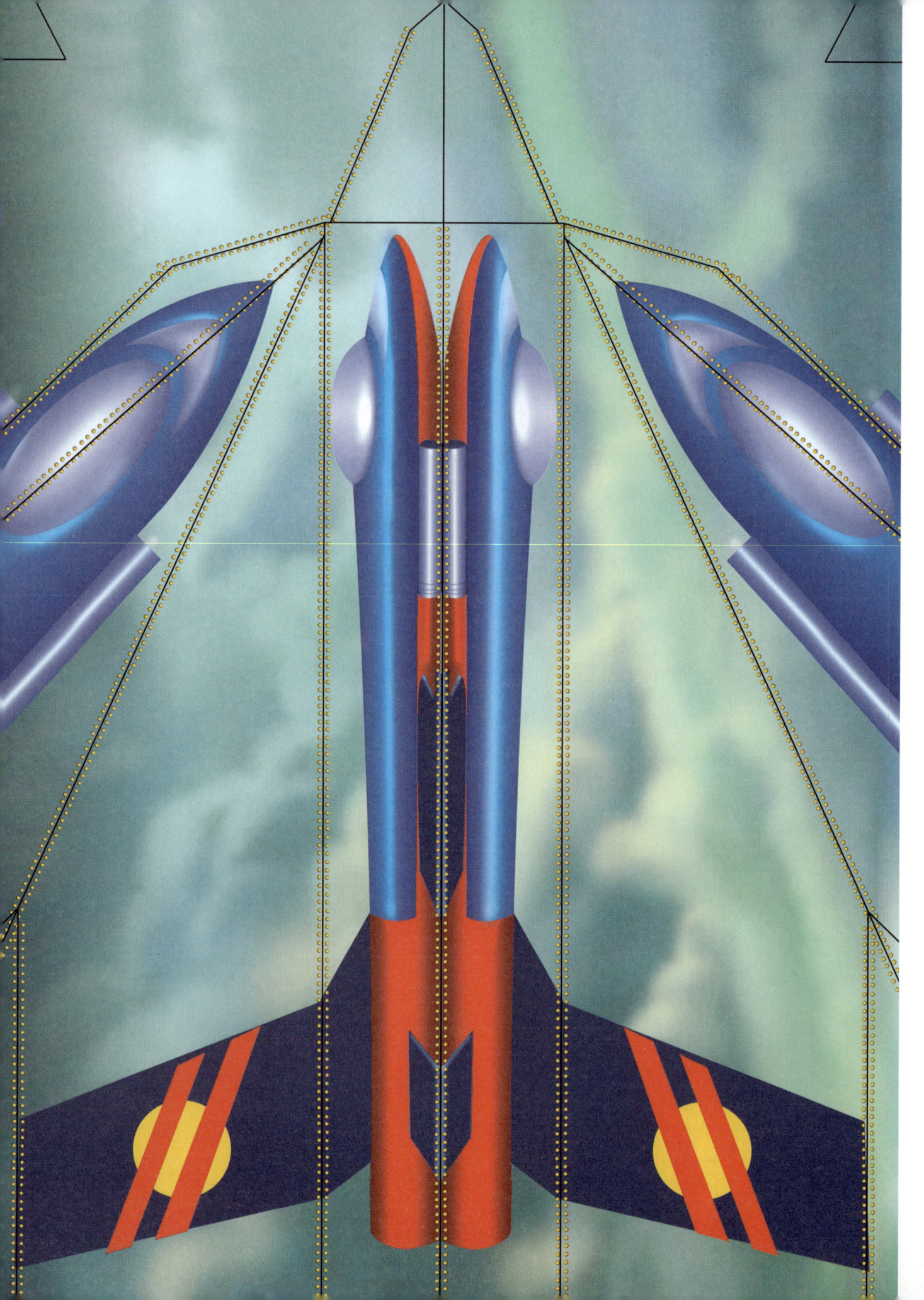

Javelin

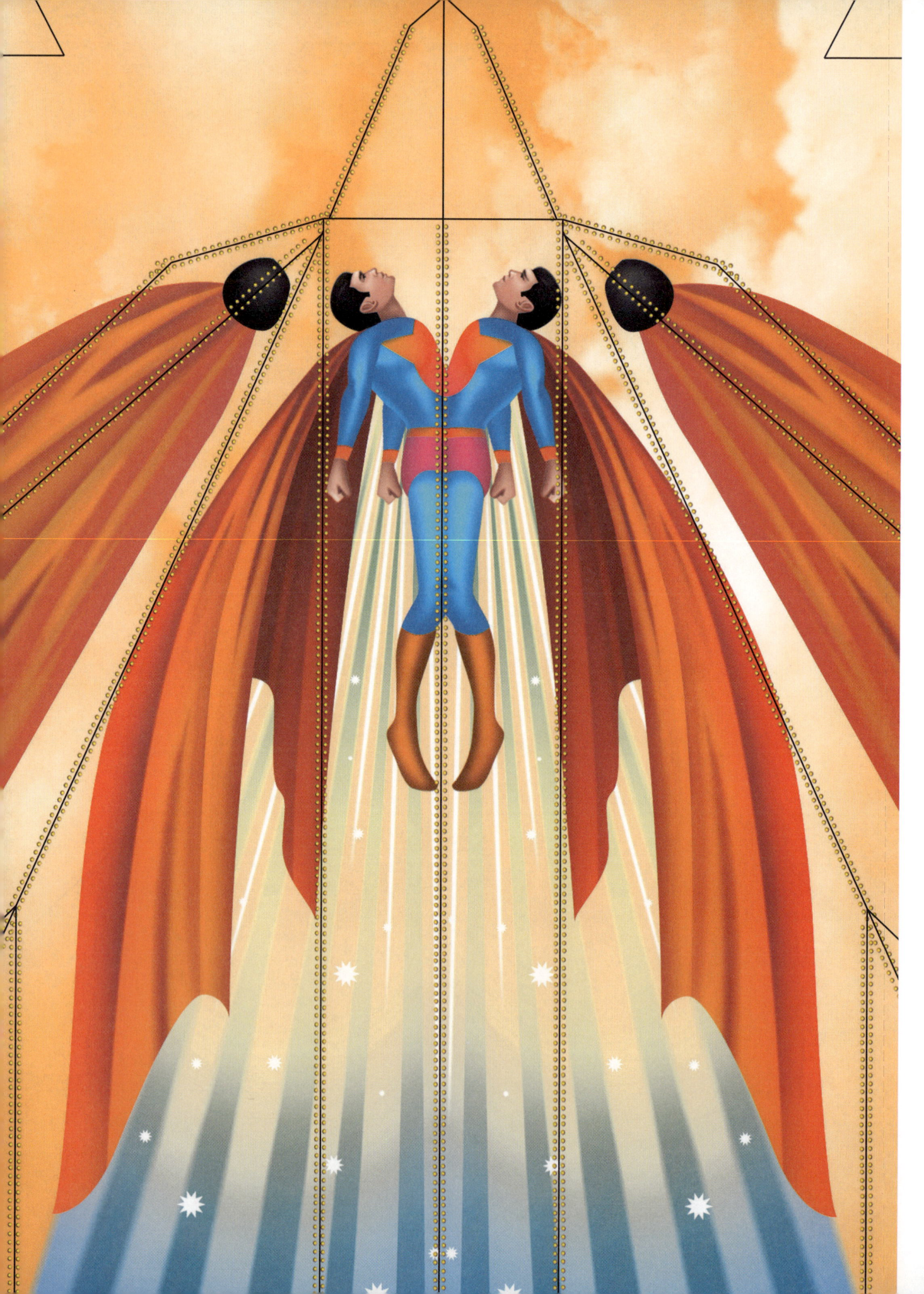

Javelin

Javelin

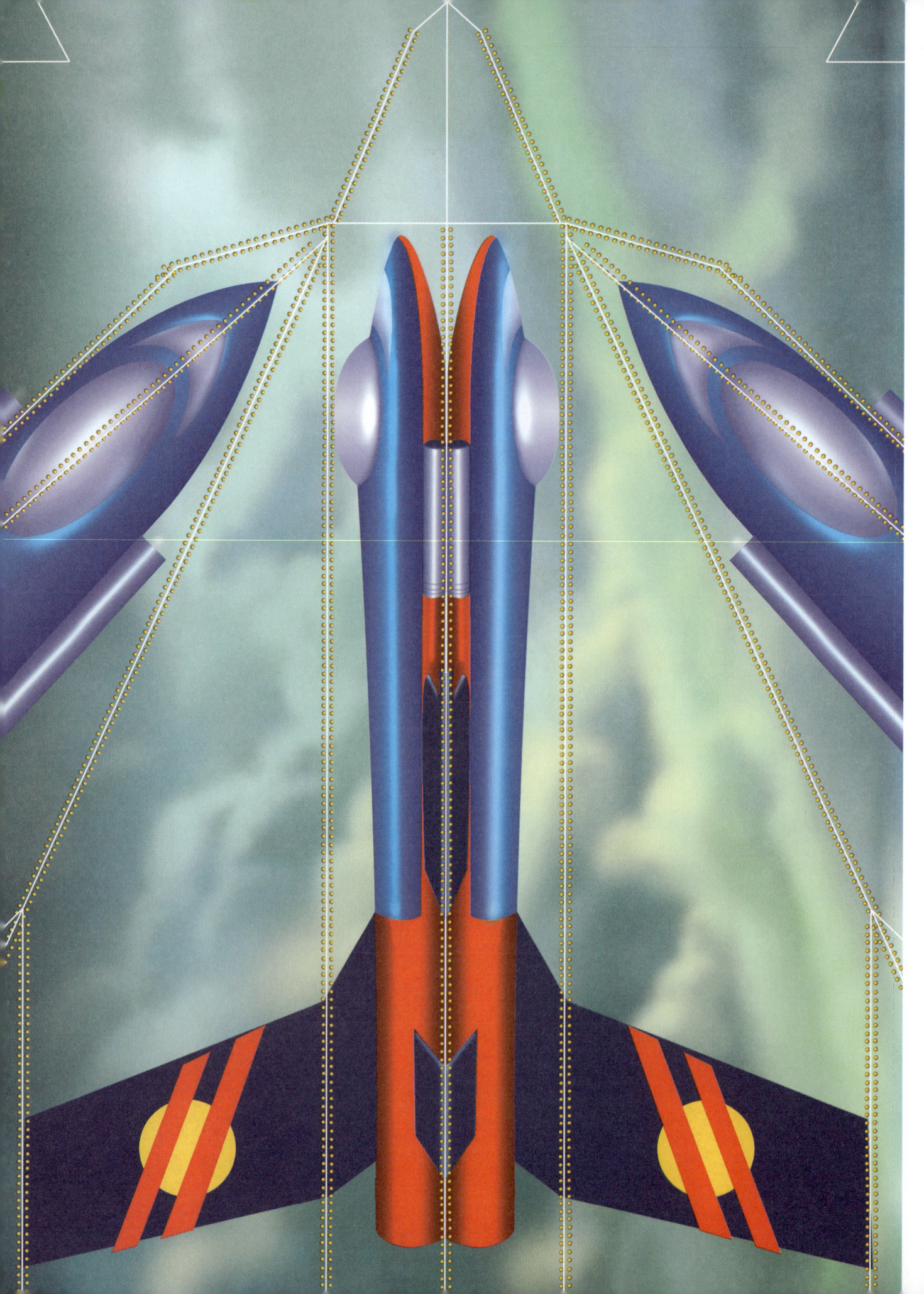

Javelin

Javelin

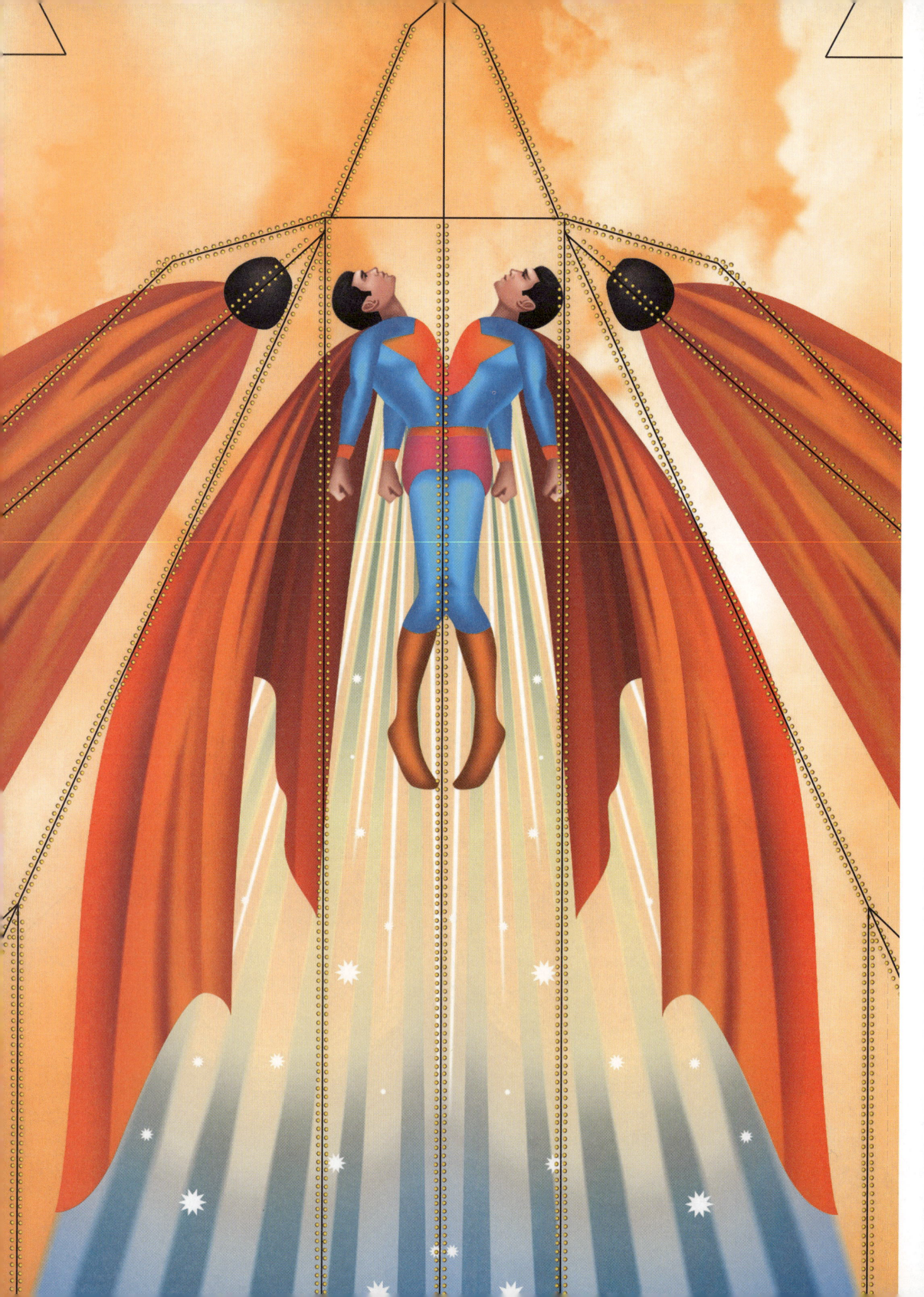

Afterburner

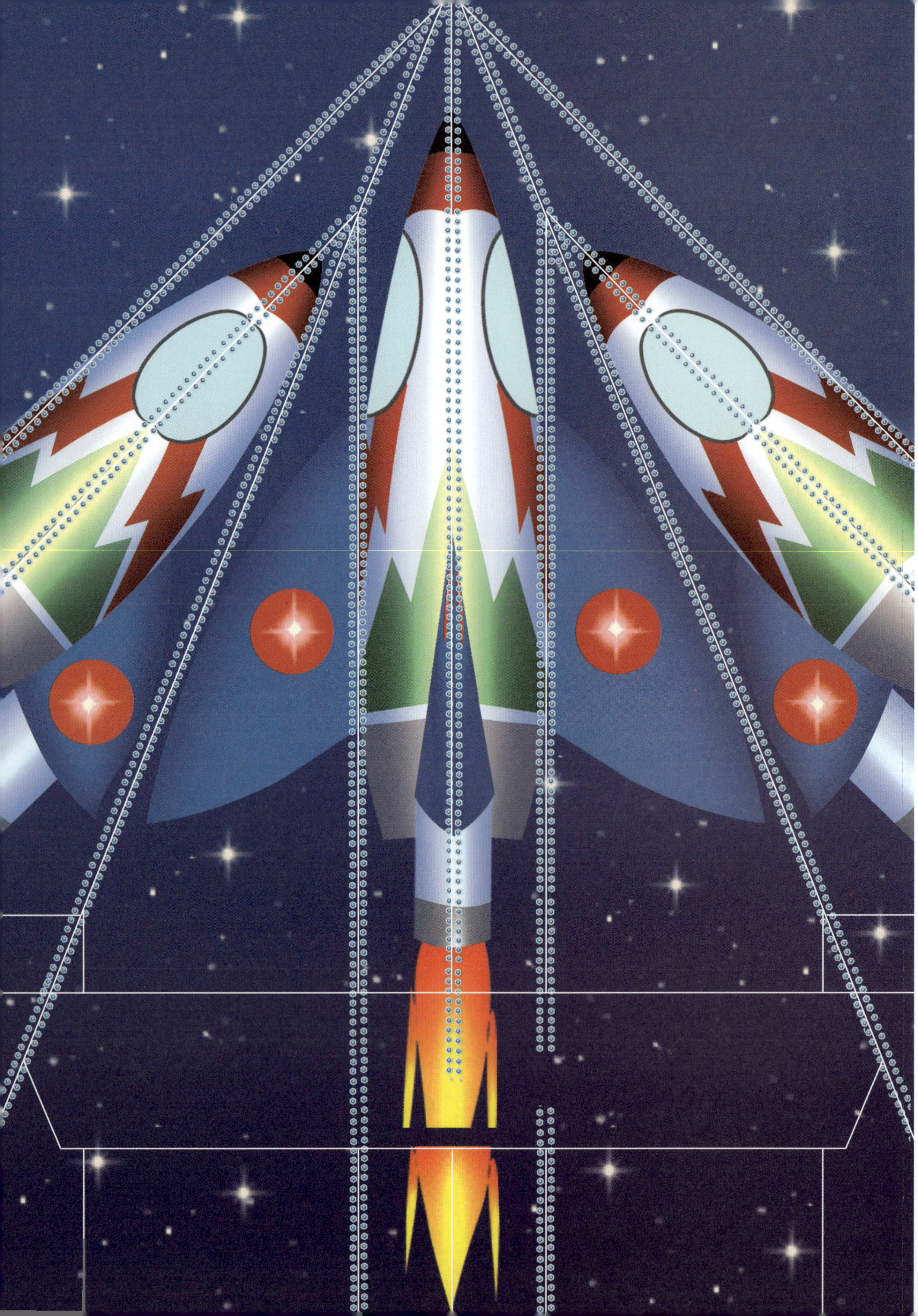

Afterburner

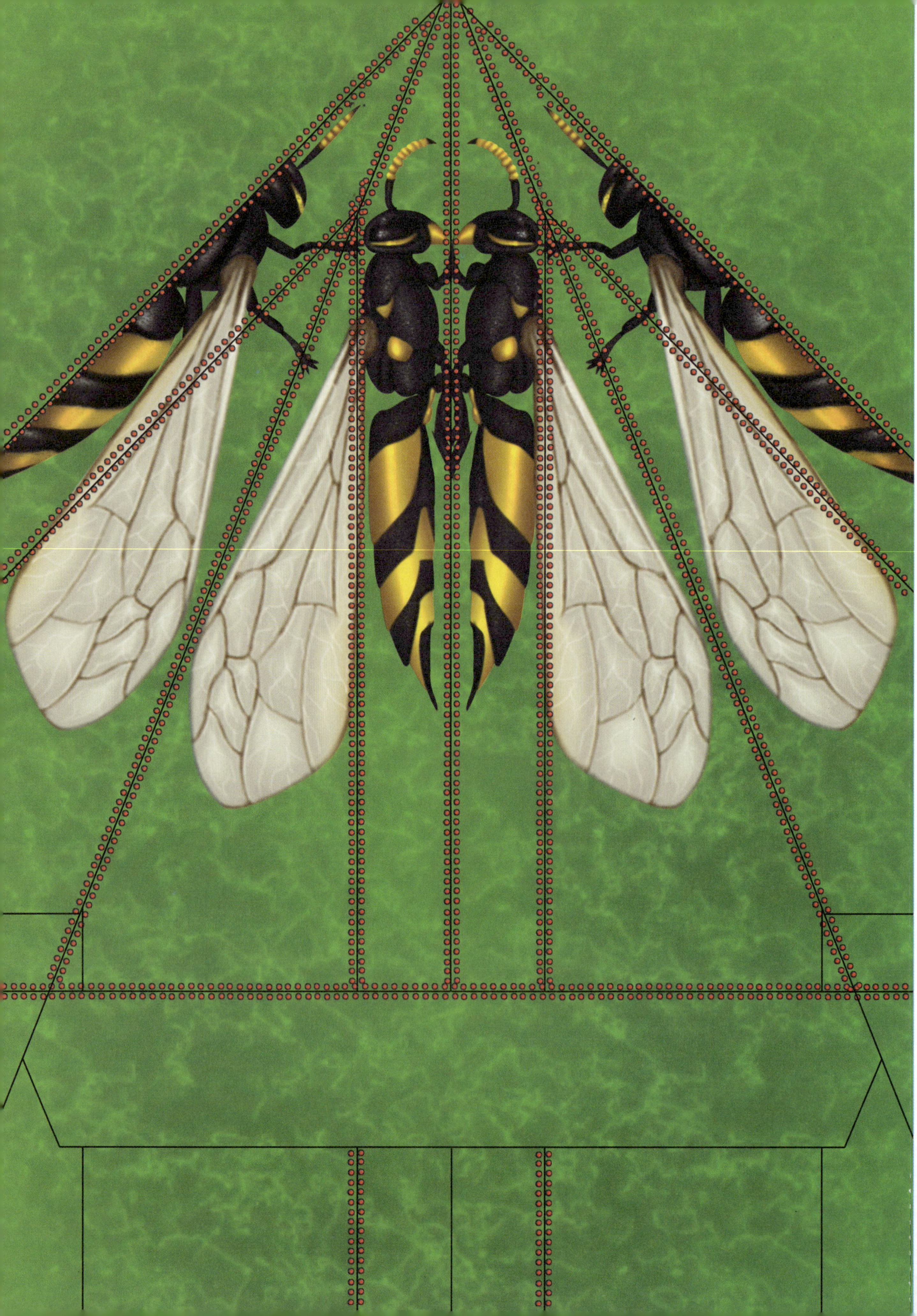

Afterburner

Afterburner

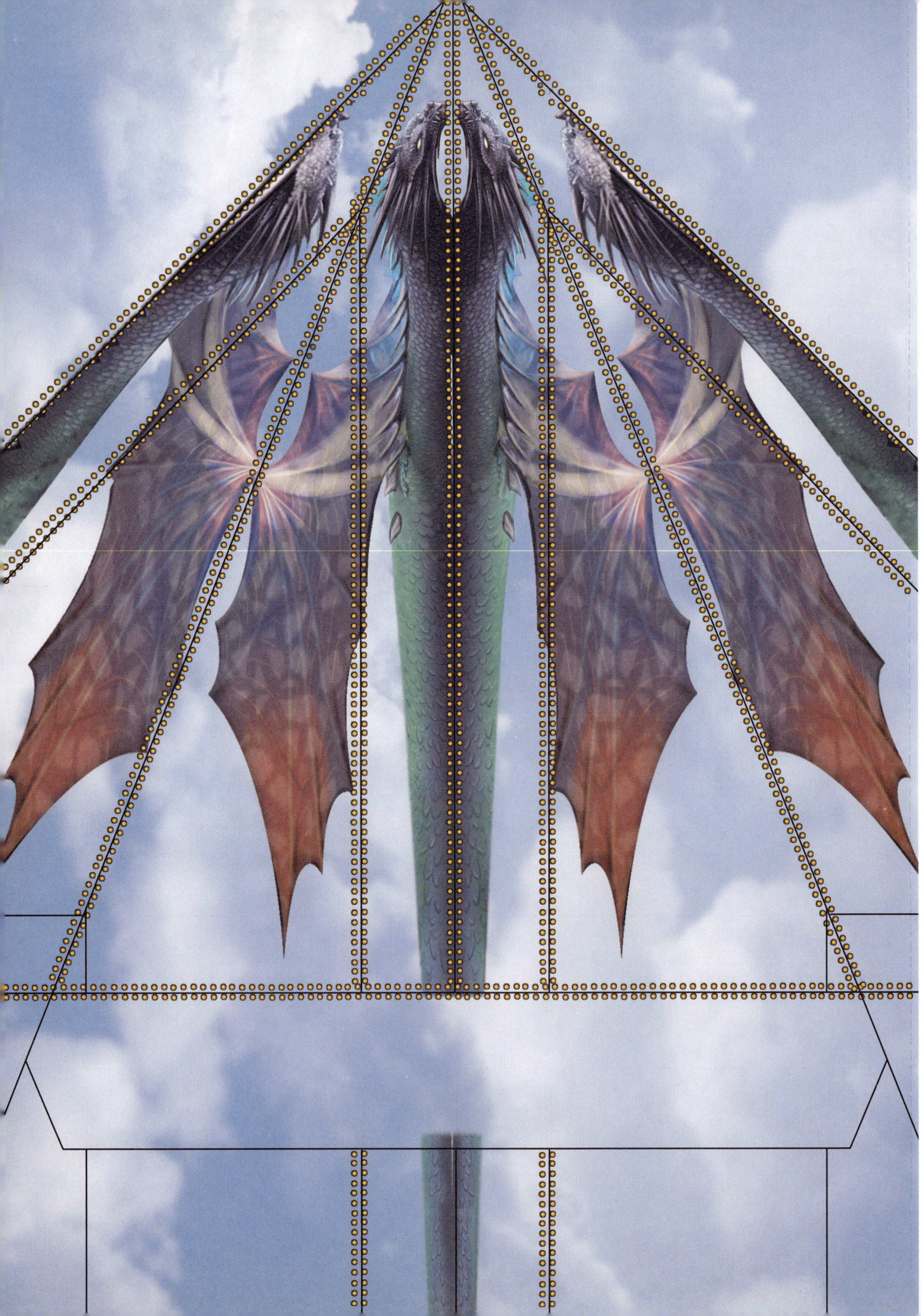

Afterburner

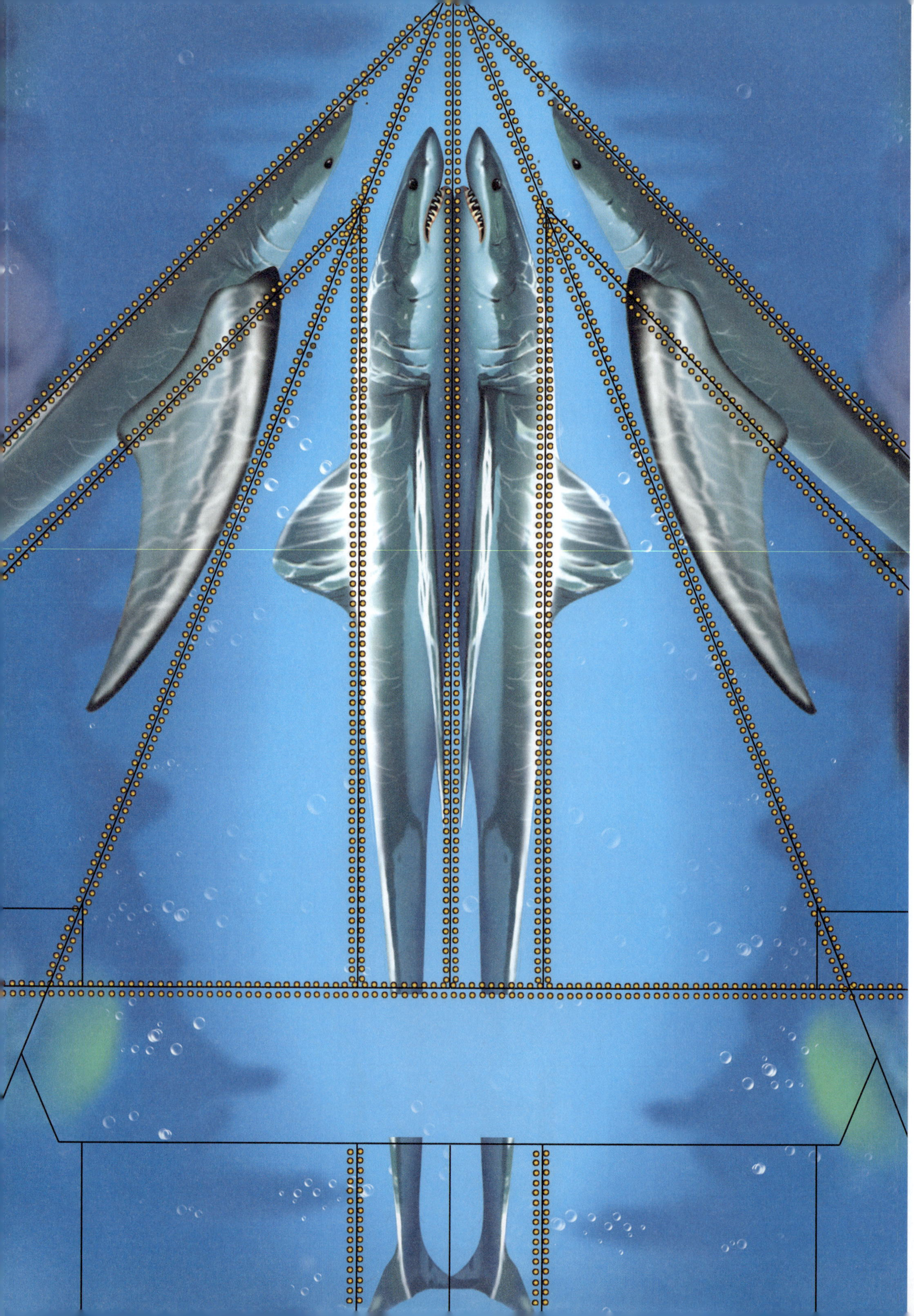

Afterburner

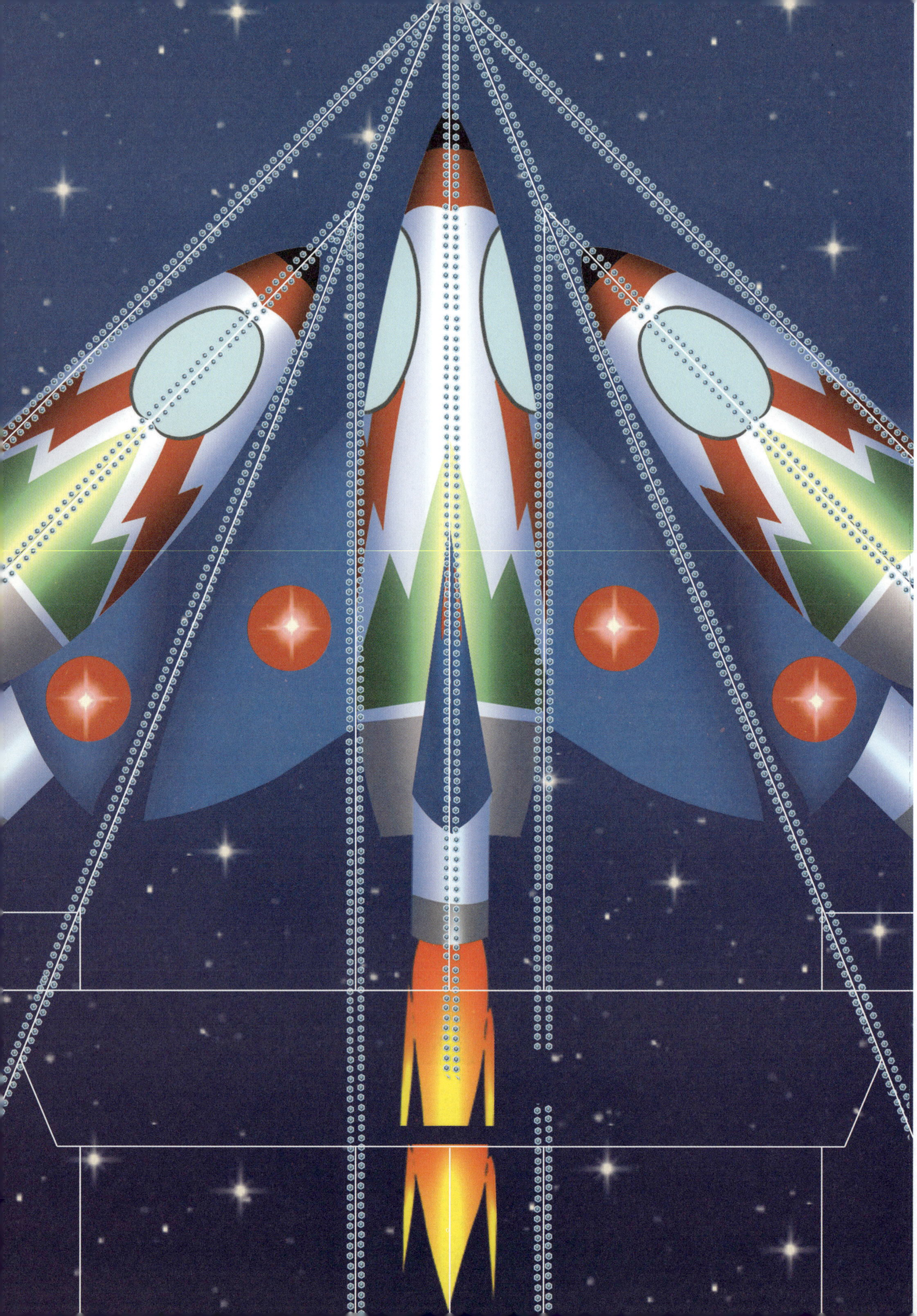

Afterburner

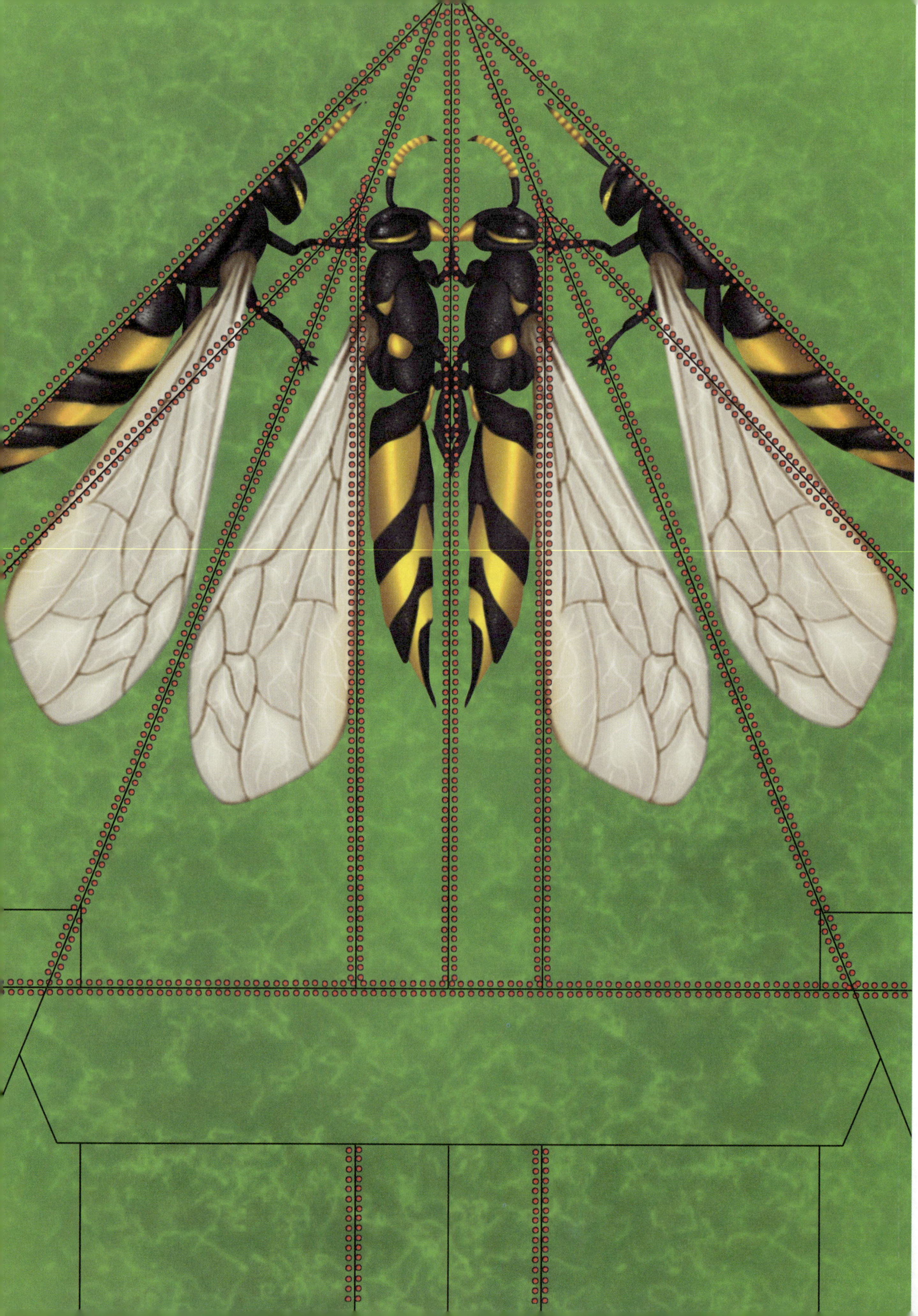

Nakamura Lock

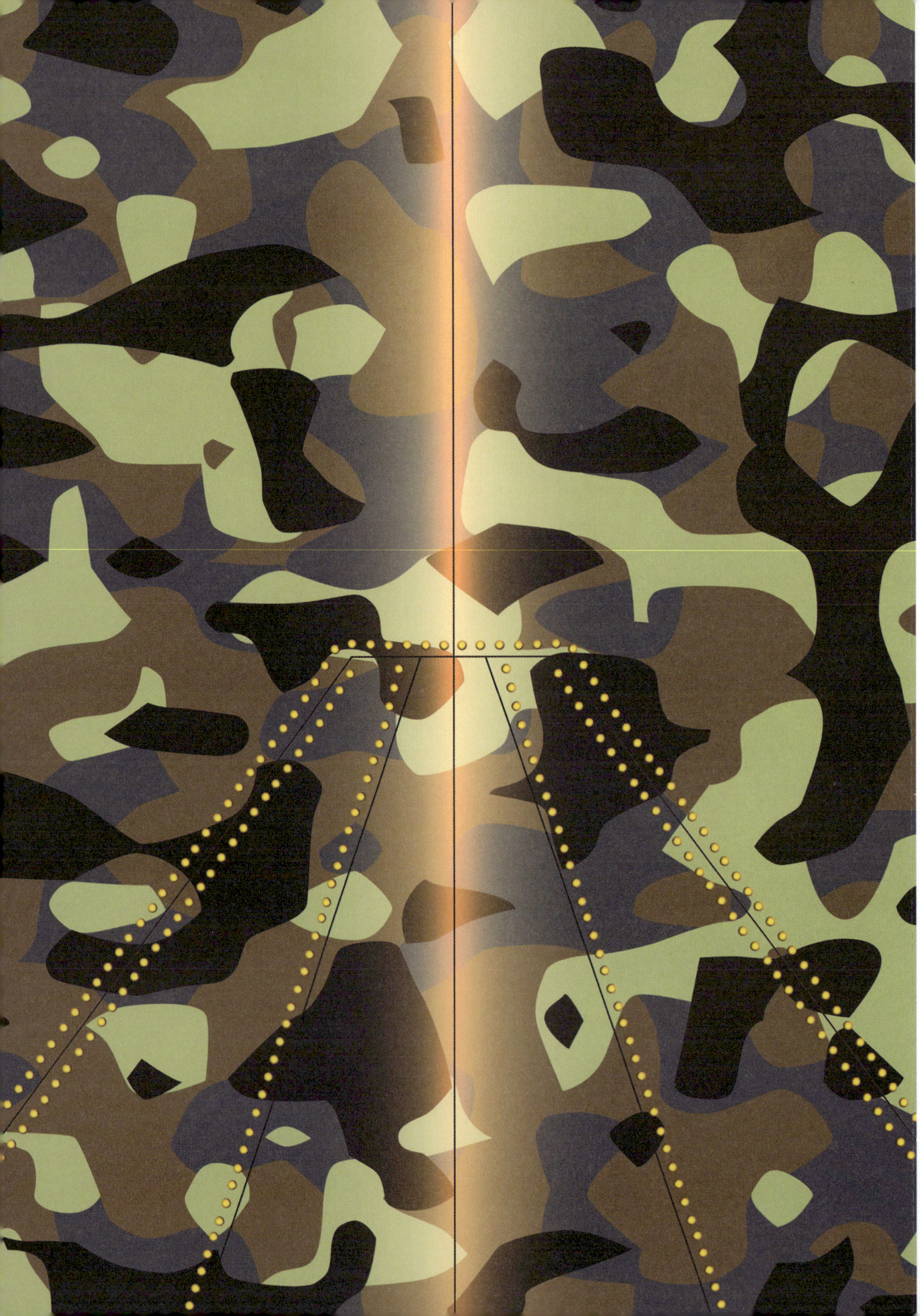

Nakamura Lock

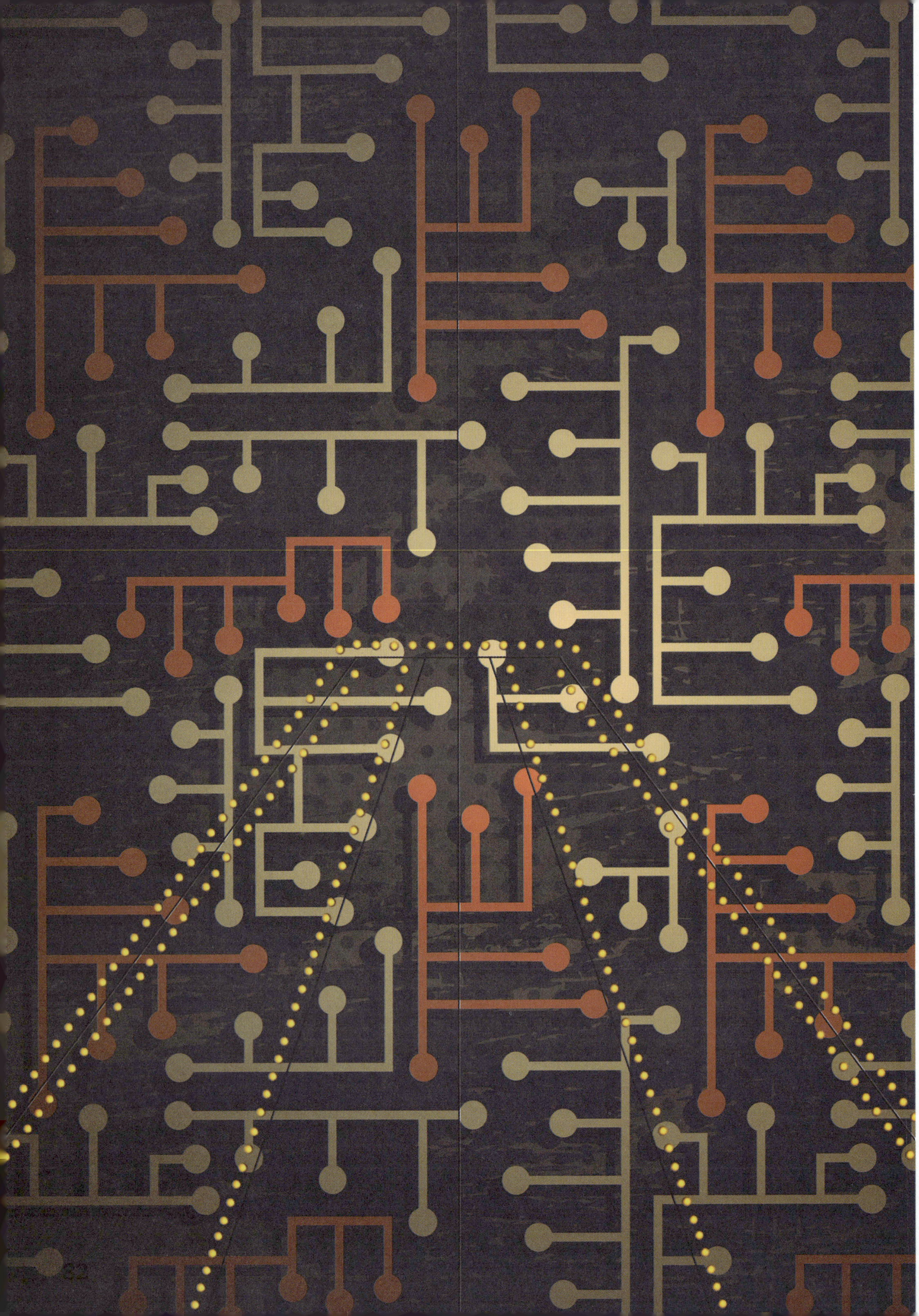

Nakamura Lock

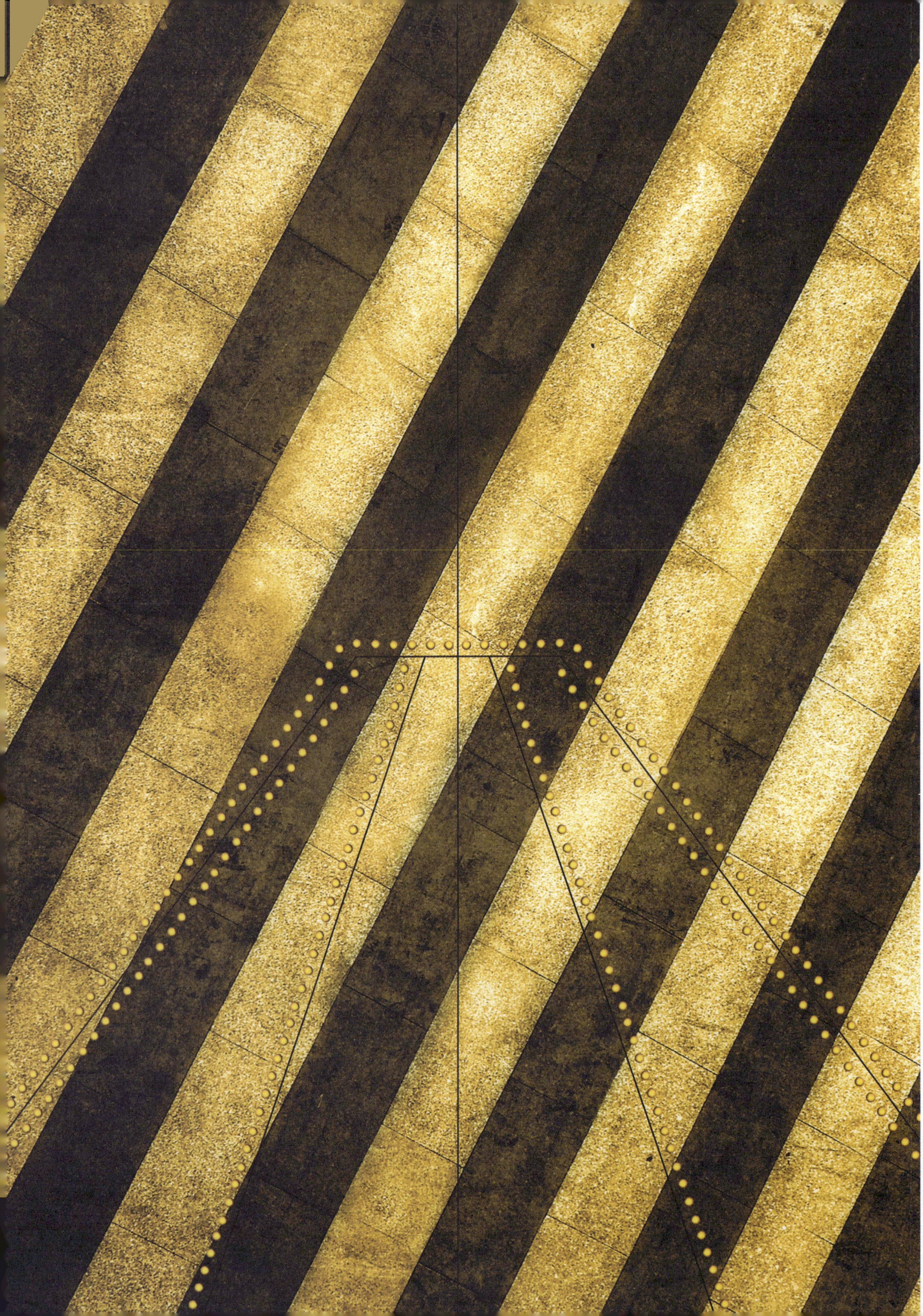

Nakamura Lock

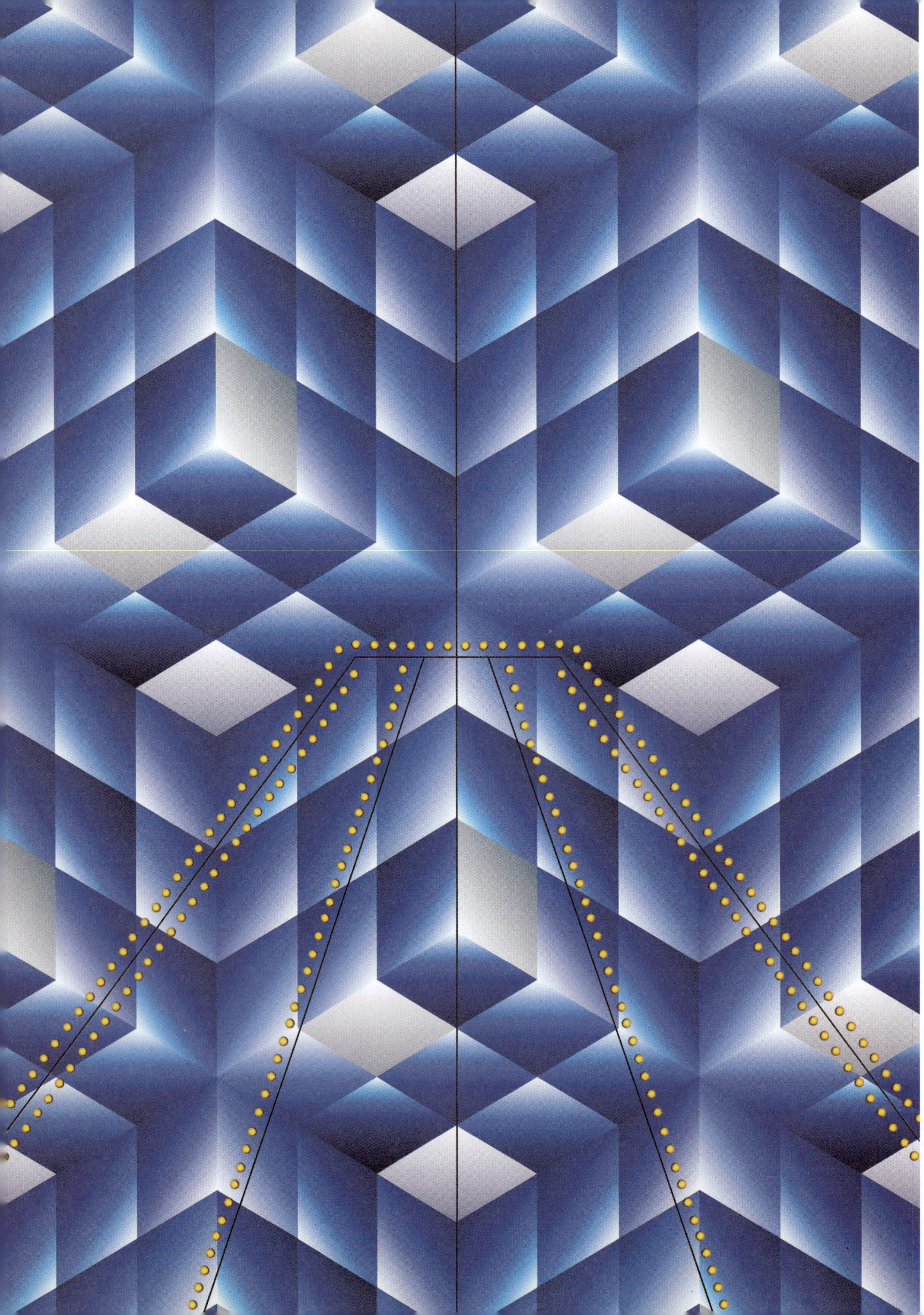

Nakamura Lock

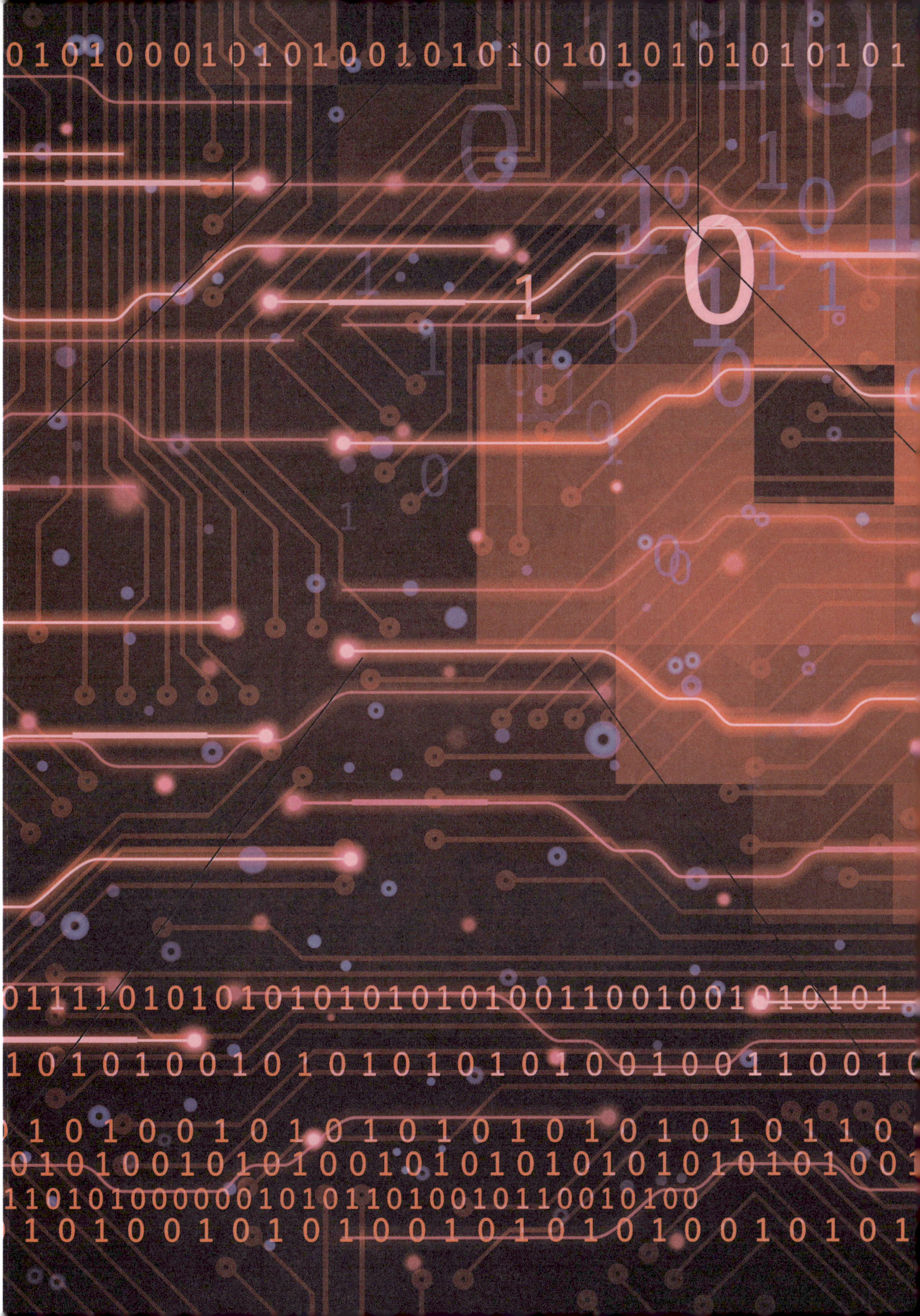

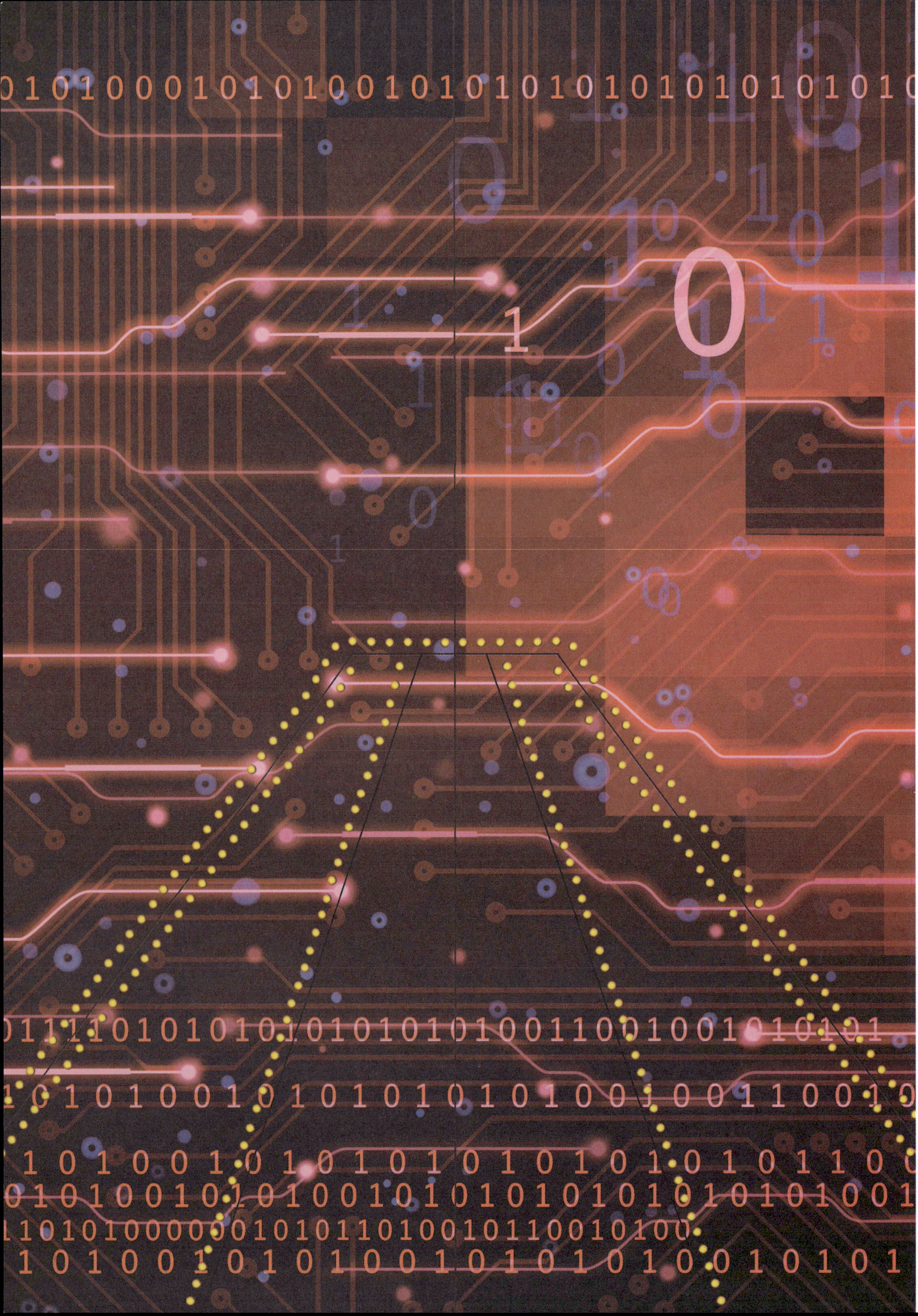

Nakamura Lock

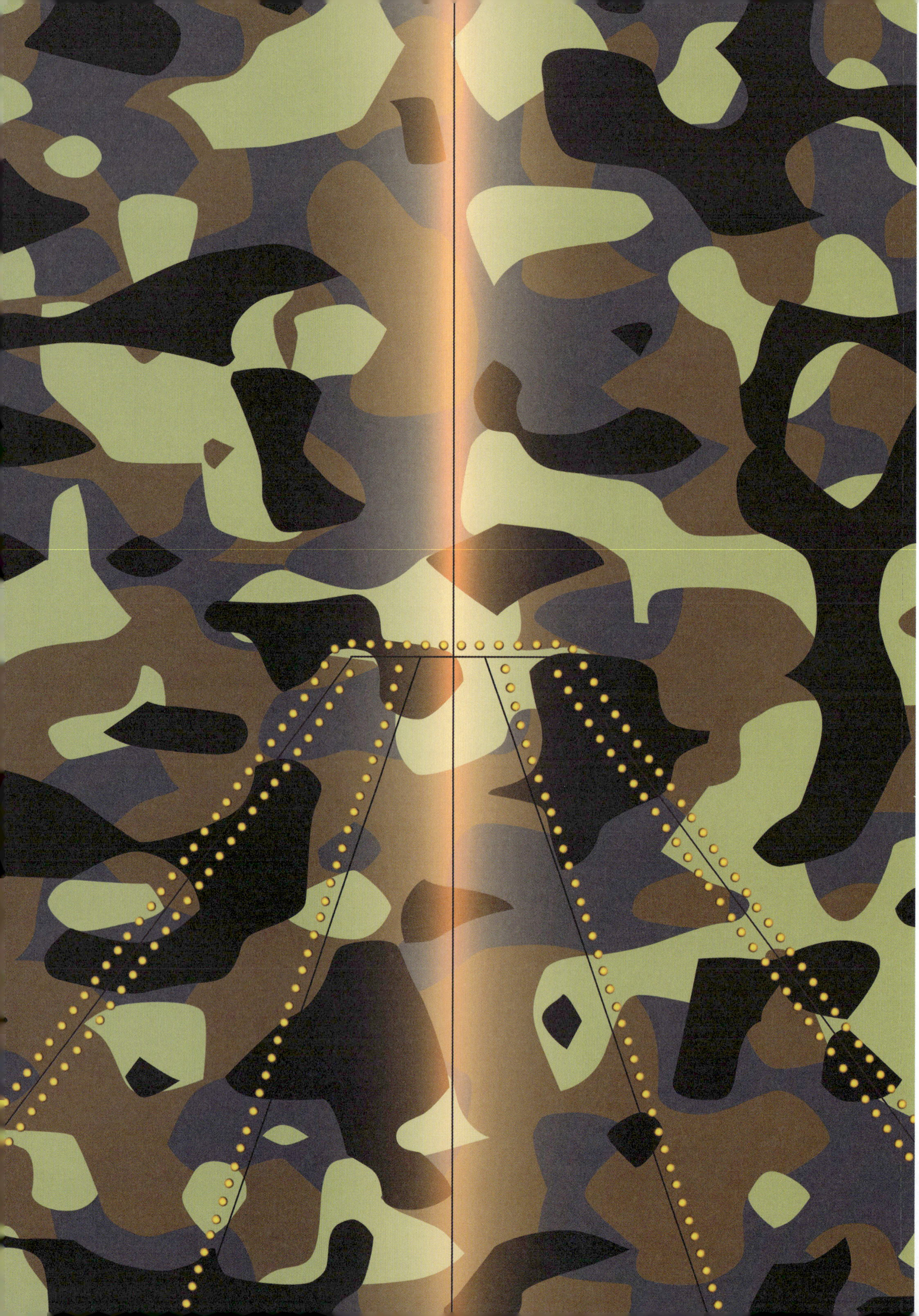

Nakamura Lock

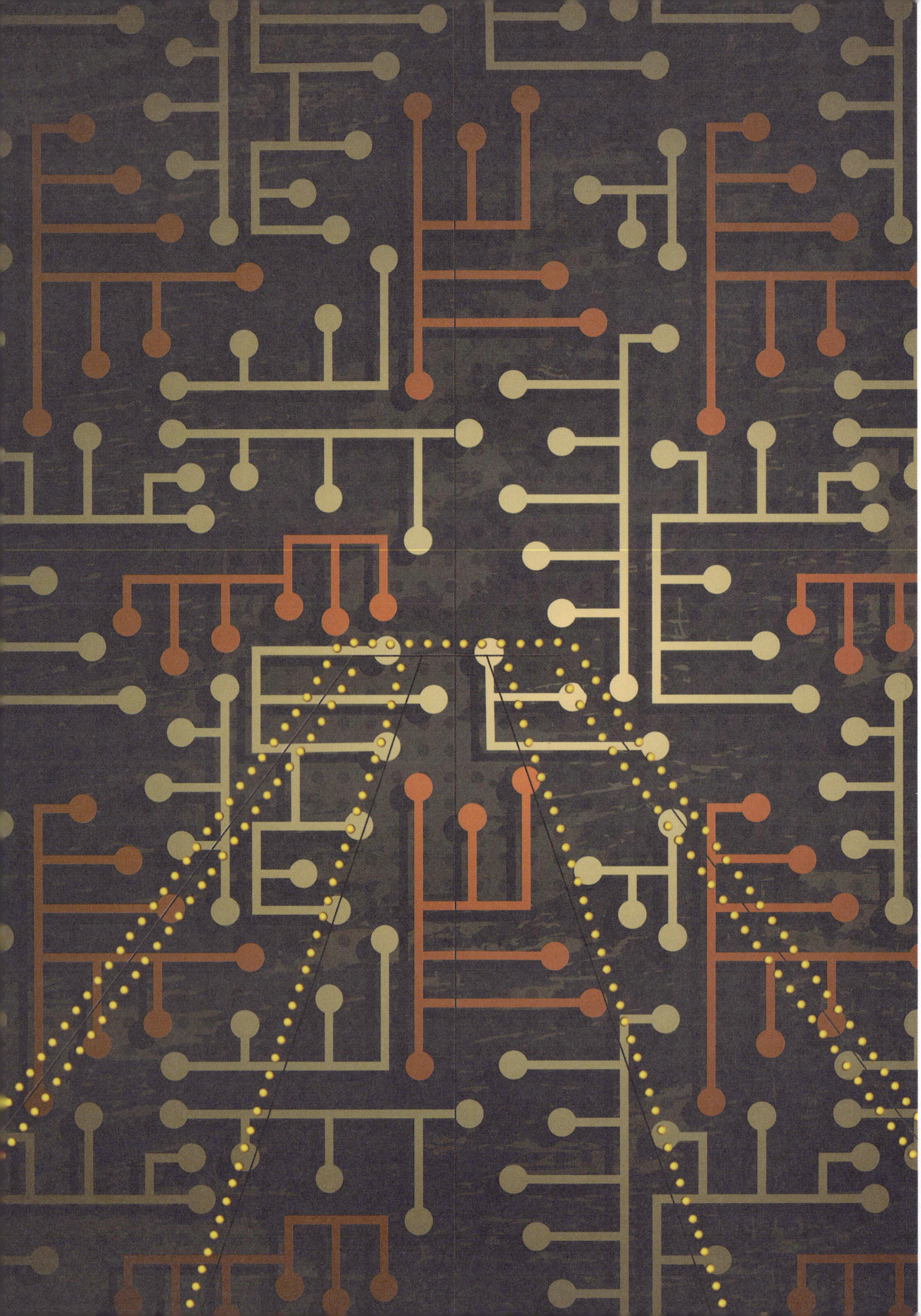

Nakamura Lock

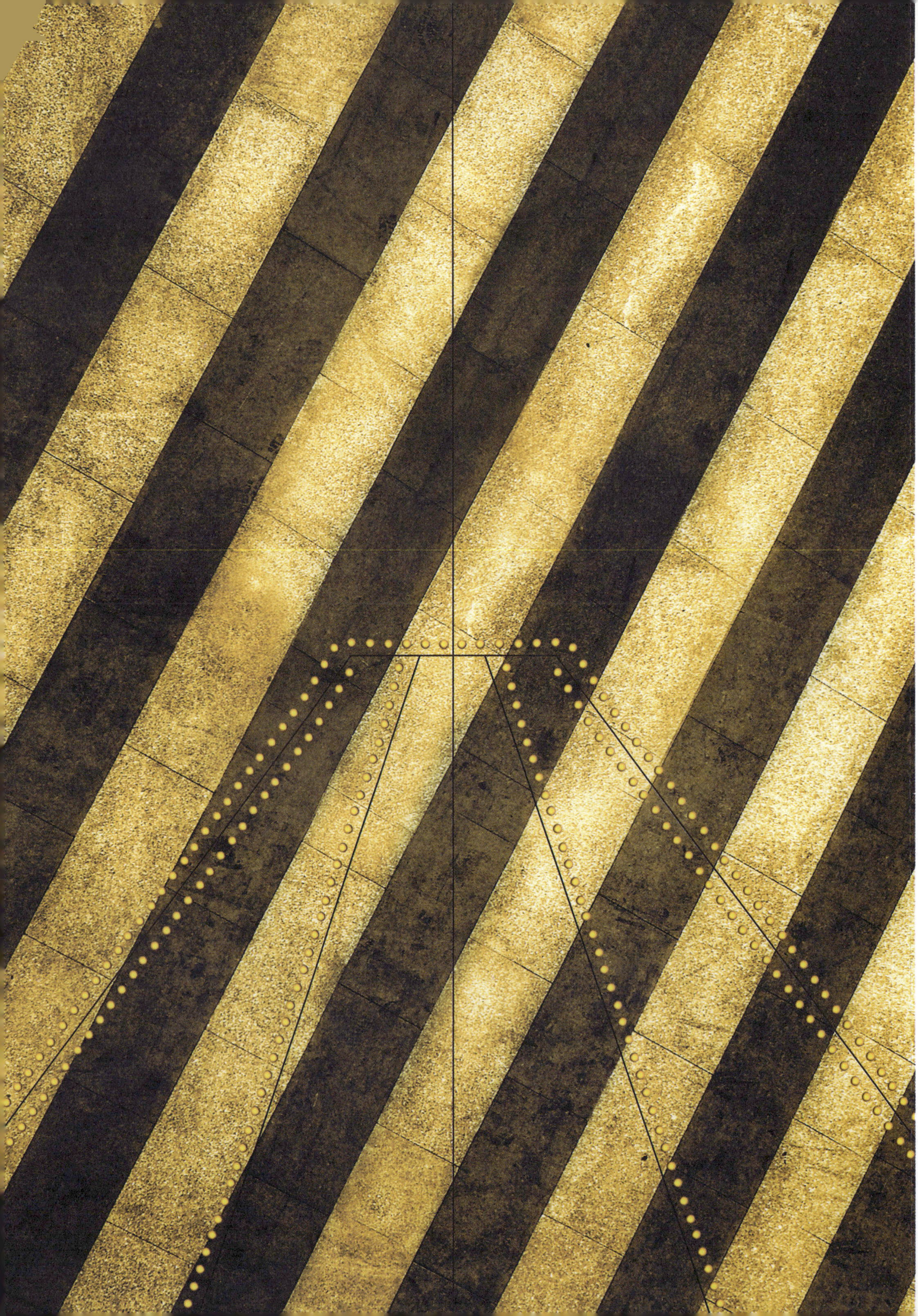

SCORING SHEETS
5-TURN GAME

PLAYER: GAME:

Game	Date	Plane	Paces	ATTEMPT					TOTAL
				1	2	3	4	5	
1									
2									
3									
4									
5									

PLAYER: GAME:

Game	Date	Plane	Paces	ATTEMPT					TOTAL
				1	2	3	4	5	
1									
2									
3									
4									
5									

PLAYER: GAME:

Game	Date	Plane	Paces	ATTEMPT					TOTAL
				1	2	3	4	5	
1									
2									
3									
4									
5									

PLAYER: GAME:

Game	Date	Plane	Paces	ATTEMPT					TOTAL
				1	2	3	4	5	
1									
2									
3									
4									
5									

5-TURN GAME

PLAYER: **GAME:**

Game	Date	Plane	Paces	ATTEMPT					TOTAL
				1	2	3	4	5	
1									
2									
3									
4									
5									

PLAYER: **GAME:**

Game	Date	Plane	Paces	ATTEMPT					TOTAL
				1	2	3	4	5	
1									
2									
3									
4									
5									

PLAYER: **GAME:**

Game	Date	Plane	Paces	ATTEMPT					TOTAL
				1	2	3	4	5	
1									
2									
3									
4									
5									

PLAYER: **GAME:**

Game	Date	Plane	Paces	ATTEMPT					TOTAL
				1	2	3	4	5	
1									
2									
3									
4									
5									

5-TURN GAME

PLAYER: GAME:

Game	Date	Plane	Paces	ATTEMPT					TOTAL
				1	2	3	4	5	
1									
2									
3									
4									
5									

PLAYER: GAME:

Game	Date	Plane	Paces	ATTEMPT					TOTAL
				1	2	3	4	5	
1									
2									
3									
4									
5									

PLAYER: GAME:

Game	Date	Plane	Paces	ATTEMPT					TOTAL
				1	2	3	4	5	
1									
2									
3									
4									
5									

PLAYER: GAME:

Game	Date	Plane	Paces	ATTEMPT					TOTAL
				1	2	3	4	5	
1									
2									
3									
4									
5									

5-TURN GAME

PLAYER: GAME:

Game	Date	Plane	Paces	ATTEMPT					TOTAL
				1	2	3	4	5	
1									
2									
3									
4									
5									

PLAYER: GAME:

Game	Date	Plane	Paces	ATTEMPT					TOTAL
				1	2	3	4	5	
1									
2									
3									
4									
5									

PLAYER: GAME:

Game	Date	Plane	Paces	ATTEMPT					TOTAL
				1	2	3	4	5	
1									
2									
3									
4									
5									

PLAYER: GAME:

Game	Date	Plane	Paces	ATTEMPT					TOTAL
				1	2	3	4	5	
1									
2									
3									
4									
5									

5-TURN GAME

PLAYER: **GAME:**

Game	Date	Plane	Paces	ATTEMPT					TOTAL
				1	2	3	4	5	
1									
2									
3									
4									
5									

PLAYER: **GAME:**

Game	Date	Plane	Paces	ATTEMPT					TOTAL
				1	2	3	4	5	
1									
2									
3									
4									
5									

PLAYER: **GAME:**

Game	Date	Plane	Paces	ATTEMPT					TOTAL
				1	2	3	4	5	
1									
2									
3									
4									
5									

PLAYER: **GAME:**

Game	Date	Plane	Paces	ATTEMPT					TOTAL
				1	2	3	4	5	
1									
2									
3									
4									
5									

5-TURN GAME

PLAYER: **GAME:**

Game	Date	Plane	Paces	ATTEMPT					TOTAL
				1	2	3	4	5	
1									
2									
3									
4									
5									

PLAYER: **GAME:**

Game	Date	Plane	Paces	ATTEMPT					TOTAL
				1	2	3	4	5	
1									
2									
3									
4									
5									

PLAYER: **GAME:**

Game	Date	Plane	Paces	ATTEMPT					TOTAL
				1	2	3	4	5	
1									
2									
3									
4									
5									

PLAYER: **GAME:**

Game	Date	Plane	Paces	ATTEMPT					TOTAL
				1	2	3	4	5	
1									
2									
3									
4									
5									

10-TURN GAME

PLAYER: **GAME:**

Game	Date	Plane	Paces	ATTEMPT											TOTAL
				1	2	3	4	5	6	7	8	9	10	
1														
2														
3														
4														
5														

PLAYER: **GAME:**

Game	Date	Plane	Paces	ATTEMPT											TOTAL
				1	2	3	4	5	6	7	8	9	10	
1														
2														
3														
4														
5														

PLAYER: **GAME:**

Game	Date	Plane	Paces	ATTEMPT											TOTAL
				1	2	3	4	5	6	7	8	9	10	
1														
2														
3														
4														
5														

PLAYER: **GAME:**

Game	Date	Plane	Paces	ATTEMPT											TOTAL
				1	2	3	4	5	6	7	8	9	10	
1														
2														
3														
4														
5														

10-TURN GAME

PLAYER: **GAME:**

Game	Date	Plane	Paces	\<ATTEMPT\> 1	2	3	4	5	6	7	8	9	10	TOTAL
1														
2														
3														
4														
5														

PLAYER: **GAME:**

Game	Date	Plane	Paces	\<ATTEMPT\> 1	2	3	4	5	6	7	8	9	10	TOTAL
1														
2														
3														
4														
5														

PLAYER: **GAME:**

Game	Date	Plane	Paces	\<ATTEMPT\> 1	2	3	4	5	6	7	8	9	10	TOTAL
1														
2														
3														
4														
5														

PLAYER: **GAME:**

Game	Date	Plane	Paces	\<ATTEMPT\> 1	2	3	4	5	6	7	8	9	10	TOTAL
1														
2														
3														
4														
5														

10-TURN GAME

PLAYER: GAME:

Game	Date	Plane	Paces	_____ ATTEMPT _____										TOTAL
				1	2	3	4	5	6	7	8	9	10	
1														
2														
3														
4														
5														

PLAYER: GAME:

Game	Date	Plane	Paces	ATTEMPT										TOTAL
				1	2	3	4	5	6	7	8	9	10	
1														
2														
3														
4														
5														

PLAYER: GAME:

Game	Date	Plane	Paces	ATTEMPT										TOTAL
				1	2	3	4	5	6	7	8	9	10	
1														
2														
3														
4														
5														

PLAYER: GAME:

Game	Date	Plane	Paces	ATTEMPT										TOTAL
				1	2	3	4	5	6	7	8	9	10	
1														
2														
3														
4														
5														

10-TURN GAME

PLAYER: GAME:

Game	Date	Plane	Paces	\multicolumn{10}{c}{ATTEMPT}	TOTAL
				1	2	3	4	5	6	7	8	9	10	
1														
2														
3														
4														
5														

PLAYER: GAME:

Game	Date	Plane	Paces	1	2	3	4	5	6	7	8	9	10	TOTAL
1														
2														
3														
4														
5														

PLAYER: GAME:

Game	Date	Plane	Paces	1	2	3	4	5	6	7	8	9	10	TOTAL
1														
2														
3														
4														
5														

PLAYER: GAME:

Game	Date	Plane	Paces	1	2	3	4	5	6	7	8	9	10	TOTAL
1														
2														
3														
4														
5														

10-TURN GAME

PLAYER: **GAME:**

Game	Date	Plane	Paces	\\multicolumn{10}{c	}{ATTEMPT}	TOTAL

Game	Date	Plane	Paces	1	2	3	4	5	6	7	8	9	10	TOTAL
1														
2														
3														
4														
5														

PLAYER: **GAME:**

Game	Date	Plane	Paces	1	2	3	4	5	6	7	8	9	10	TOTAL
1														
2														
3														
4														
5														

PLAYER: **GAME:**

Game	Date	Plane	Paces	1	2	3	4	5	6	7	8	9	10	TOTAL
1														
2														
3														
4														
5														

PLAYER: **GAME:**

Game	Date	Plane	Paces	1	2	3	4	5	6	7	8	9	10	TOTAL
1														
2														
3														
4														
5														

10-TURN GAME

PLAYER: **GAME:**

Game	Date	Plane	Paces	\multicolumn{10}{c}{ATTEMPT}	TOTAL
				1	2	3	4	5	6	7	8	9	10	
1														
2														
3														
4														
5														

PLAYER: **GAME:**

Game	Date	Plane	Paces	ATTEMPT										TOTAL
				1	2	3	4	5	6	7	8	9	10	
1														
2														
3														
4														
5														

PLAYER: **GAME:**

Game	Date	Plane	Paces	ATTEMPT										TOTAL
				1	2	3	4	5	6	7	8	9	10	
1														
2														
3														
4														
5														

PLAYER: **GAME:**

Game	Date	Plane	Paces	ATTEMPT										TOTAL
				1	2	3	4	5	6	7	8	9	10	
1														
2														
3														
4														
5														

PLANE POOL

PLAYER:

Game	BALL SUNK							
	1	2	3	4	5	6	7	8
1								
2								
3								
4								
5								

PLAYER:

Game	BALL SUNK							
	1	2	3	4	5	6	7	8
1								
2								
3								
4								
5								

PLAYER:

Game	BALL SUNK							
	1	2	3	4	5	6	7	8
1								
2								
3								
4								
5								

PLAYER:

Game	BALL SUNK							
	1	2	3	4	5	6	7	8
1								
2								
3								
4								
5								

PLAYER:

Game	BALL SUNK							
	1	2	3	4	5	6	7	8
1								
2								
3								
4								
5								

PLAYER:

Game	BALL SUNK							
	1	2	3	4	5	6	7	8
1								
2								
3								
4								
5								

PLAYER:

Game	BALL SUNK							
	1	2	3	4	5	6	7	8
1								
2								
3								
4								
5								

PLAYER:

Game	BALL SUNK							
	1	2	3	4	5	6	7	8
1								
2								
3								
4								
5								

PLANE POOL

PLAYER:

Game	BALL SUNK							
	1	2	3	4	5	6	7	8
1								
2								
3								
4								
5								

PLAYER:

Game	BALL SUNK							
	1	2	3	4	5	6	7	8
1								
2								
3								
4								
5								

PLAYER:

Game	BALL SUNK							
	1	2	3	4	5	6	7	8
1								
2								
3								
4								
5								

PLAYER:

Game	BALL SUNK							
	1	2	3	4	5	6	7	8
1								
2								
3								
4								
5								

PLAYER:

Game	BALL SUNK							
	1	2	3	4	5	6	7	8
1								
2								
3								
4								
5								

PLAYER:

Game	BALL SUNK							
	1	2	3	4	5	6	7	8
1								
2								
3								
4								
5								

PLAYER:

Game	BALL SUNK							
	1	2	3	4	5	6	7	8
1								
2								
3								
4								
5								

PLAYER:

Game	BALL SUNK							
	1	2	3	4	5	6	7	8
1								
2								
3								
4								
5								

PLANE POOL

PLAYER:

Game	BALL SUNK							
	1	2	3	4	5	6	7	8
1								
2								
3								
4								
5								

PLAYER:

Game	BALL SUNK							
	1	2	3	4	5	6	7	8
1								
2								
3								
4								
5								

PLAYER:

Game	BALL SUNK							
	1	2	3	4	5	6	7	8
1								
2								
3								
4								
5								

PLAYER:

Game	BALL SUNK							
	1	2	3	4	5	6	7	8
1								
2								
3								
4								
5								

PLAYER:

Game	BALL SUNK							
	1	2	3	4	5	6	7	8
1								
2								
3								
4								
5								

PLAYER:

Game	BALL SUNK							
	1	2	3	4	5	6	7	8
1								
2								
3								
4								
5								

PLAYER:

Game	BALL SUNK							
	1	2	3	4	5	6	7	8
1								
2								
3								
4								
5								

PLAYER:

Game	BALL SUNK							
	1	2	3	4	5	6	7	8
1								
2								
3								
4								
5								

PLANE POOL

PLAYER:

Game	BALL SUNK							
	1	2	3	4	5	6	7	8
1								
2								
3								
4								
5								

PLAYER:

Game	BALL SUNK							
	1	2	3	4	5	6	7	8
1								
2								
3								
4								
5								

PLAYER:

Game	BALL SUNK							
	1	2	3	4	5	6	7	8
1								
2								
3								
4								
5								

PLAYER:

Game	BALL SUNK							
	1	2	3	4	5	6	7	8
1								
2								
3								
4								
5								

PLAYER:

Game	BALL SUNK							
	1	2	3	4	5	6	7	8
1								
2								
3								
4								
5								

PLAYER:

Game	BALL SUNK							
	1	2	3	4	5	6	7	8
1								
2								
3								
4								
5								

PLAYER:

Game	BALL SUNK							
	1	2	3	4	5	6	7	8
1								
2								
3								
4								
5								

PLAYER:

Game	BALL SUNK							
	1	2	3	4	5	6	7	8
1								
2								
3								
4								
5								